Rome and Its Empire, AD 193–284

DEBATES AND DOCUMENTS IN ANCIENT HISTORY

GENERAL EDITORS

Emma Stafford, *University of Leeds*, and
Shaun Tougher, *Cardiff University*

Focusing on important themes, events or periods throughout ancient
history, each volume in this series is divided into roughly equal parts.
The first introduces the reader to the main issues of interpretation.
The second contains a selection of relevant evidence supporting
different views.

PUBLISHED

Diocletian and the Tetrarchy
Roger Rees

Julian the Apostate
Shaun Tougher

Rome and Its Empire, AD 193–284
Olivier Hekster with Nicholas Zair

IN PREPARATION

Roman Imperialism
Andrew Erskine

Sex and Sexuality in Classical Athens
James Robson

The Emperor Nero
Steven Green

Justinian and the Sixth Century
Fiona Haarer

Rome and Its Empire, AD 193–284

Olivier Hekster with Nicholas Zair

Edinburgh University Press

© Olivier Hekster, 2008

Edinburgh University Press Ltd
22 George Square, Edinburgh

Typeset in Minion
by Norman Tilley Graphics Ltd, Northampton
and printed and bound in Great Britain
by CPI Antony Rowe, Chippenham, Wilts

A CIP record for this book is available from the British Library

ISBN 978 0 7486 2303 7 (hardback)
ISBN 978 0 7486 2304 4 (paperback)

The right of Olivier Hekster
to be identified as author of this work
has been asserted in accordance with
the Copyright, Designs and Patents Act 1988.

Contents

Series Editors' Preface

Debates and Documents in Ancient History is a series of short books on central topics in Greek and Roman history. It will range over the whole period of classical history from the early first millennium BC to the sixth century AD. The works in the series are written by expert academics and provide up-to-date and accessible accounts of the historical issues and problems raised by each topic. They also contain the important evidence on which the arguments are based, including texts (in translation), archaeological data and visual material. This allows readers to judge how convincing the arguments are and to enter the debates themselves. The series is intended for all those interested in the history of the Greek and Roman world.

In this volume Olivier Hekster explores in particular the condition of the Roman empire in the third century AD, prior to the emergence of the dominating figure of the emperor Diocletian (AD 284–305). This period has been categorised as one of crisis for the empire, since it witnessed intense political, social, economic, military and religious upheaval. Most obviously the empire experienced severe imperial instability and pressure on its northern and eastern frontiers. However, the degree of crisis the empire was facing is a matter for lively debate, which makes it an ideal topic for this series. In addition, one of the key problems facing historians of the third century AD is the lack of primary evidence. Olivier Hekster thus provides a vital service in bringing together in one volume a range of literary and material evidence on which interpretations of the period can be based, such as histories, speeches, oracles, inscriptions, Christian tracts, papyri, legislation, letters, monuments, statues and coins. He draws on all of these to provide a thoughtful and balanced consideration of Rome's history from AD 193 to 284. This volume should provide an invaluable tool for students, teachers and all those interested in the history of the Roman Empire.

Emma Stafford and Shaun Tougher
November 2007

Preface

Large stretches of the monumental walls with which the emperor Aurelian surrounded the city of Rome are still standing. Nowadays, they are an imposing relic of the greatness of imperial Rome. Yet the decision in AD 271 that the city needed walls marks an important moment in Roman history. The empire could no longer guarantee peace in its heartland. The period between AD 193 and 284 is often described as a time of crisis, an era in which everything went wrong that possibly could have gone wrong. But even after years of near-continuous fighting, in spite of everything, Rome and its empire had survived almost entirely intact. When Diocletian took up power in AD 284, the Roman Empire was in many ways still the same as it had been at the end of the second century. There was change, of course, but continuity too. The third century is a confusing period of Roman history, in which events took place at an incredible pace, major battles were lost but wars were won, and two of the most recognisable legacies of Roman history came to full growth: Christianity and Roman law. After years of relative neglect, it is also a period which now receives academic attention. Historians ask new questions, or give different answers to old ones, partly by using different sources from those earlier scholars had access to. These historians, as so often, disagree with one another, giving rise to fierce debates. This books aims to highlight some debates relating to Rome and its empire, and the ancient sources that are referred to in these debates.

Since so much happens in the 'short third century' (the ninety-one years from AD 193 to 284), Part I (Debates) starts with an introduction which very briefly discusses the main events of the times, in Rome and its empire, followed by a short presentation of the main sources. Here one can find the first cross-referencing to the sources in Part II (Documents). Throughout Part I, cross-references to the sources under discussion are indicated by bold type in brackets: for example (**II. 5**) refers to the fifth section in part II, and (**II. 5 9.1**) refers to a subsection (9.1) within that fifth section. References to modern literature are indicated (also in brackets) by author and year of publication. The bibliography supplies further details. In some cases, references are made to ancient sources which are not in Part II. These are also in brackets. Maps (pp. xv–xvii) and a list of emperors and usurpers with their years of reign (pp. 155–6) may also be of help.

Part I is divided into five chapters, each dealing with an important theme in third-century history. Though it elaborates to some extent on the narrative framework given in the introduction, especially in the first two chapters, it does not aim to supply a full overview of events. The guide to further reading which follows Part II gives directions on where to look for more information. Instead, Part I introduces some of the main debates surrounding Rome and its empire, and aims to give the background that is necessary to follow the debates. Continuously, the sources which are of importance to understand the third century are discussed and explained, hopefully in a way which makes both the debates and the documents more comprehensible to the reader. Inevitably, a short book like this has to exclude much that is relevant to the subject, in both parts. Especially regrettable was the need to omit, for reasons of space, events outside of the Roman world. That does not deny the importance of understanding how and why external threats increased as much as they did during the third century. Again, some references can be found in the guide to further reading. Also for reasons of space, almost all of third-century philosophy has been left out. The debate on whether or not there was a third-century crisis is only briefly discussed in the conclusion.

This book would never have arrived at the press in time (if at all) without Nicholas Zair, who is responsible for almost all of the translations, and whose good humour and accuracy have been a great support. Only very few of the translations have been expanded or slightly adapted by me. For the Thirteenth Sibylline Oracle (**II. 9**) I have used the translation by David Potter (Potter 1990), and am most grateful to him for his permission to reproduce it. The translation of the *Res Gestae Divi Saporis* (**II. 10**) is by Richard Frye (Frye 1984). I thank both him and the publishers, Beck, for their permission to use it. Freke Remmers has helped me at various stages of the editorial process, and I am thankful to her, as I am to Carol MacDonald at Edinburgh University Press, and to the series editors Shaun Tougher and Emma Stafford, without whom this book would not have been written. In obtaining the right maps and images I have received kind help from John Nichols, Jon Coulston, Nathalie de Haan, Maria Brosius and Ted Kaizer, the last of whom also read (and improved) parts of the text. I am grateful to the Deutsches Archäologisches Institut Rom (DAIR), the Ny Carlsberg Glyptotek, the Martin von Wagner Museum and the Compagnie Generale de Bourse (CGB) for their permission to use images from their collections. If the book serves its purpose, that is in no small part thanks to the third-century research group at Nijmegen. Lukas de Blois, Daniëlle Slootjes, Martijn Icks, Erika Manders, Inge Mennen and (our temporary resident) Matthias Haake have taught me most of what I know about the third century. Most of all, however, I am grateful to Hannah for delaying the publication of this book, first by being born, and then by distracting me as much as she could; and to Birgit, for taking care of both of us when I needed to be at the library or in my study, and for so much more.

Olivier Hekster
Arnhem, July 2007

Acknowledgements

Grateful acknowledgement is made to the following sources for permission to reproduce material. Every effort has been made to trace the copyright holders, but if any have been inadvertently overlooked, the publisher will be pleased to make the necessary arrangements at the first opportunity.

Map 1 Map © copyright 2007, Ancient World Mapping Centre
       (www.unc.edu/awmc)
Map 2 Map © copyright 2007, Ancient World Mapping Centre
       (www.unc.edu/awmc)
Map 3 Courtesy of J. Nichols/University of Oregon
       (darkwing.uoregon.edu/~atlas
Map 4 Courtesy of J. Nichols/University of Oregon
       (darkwing.uoregon.edu/~atlas)

II. 9   Translation by David Potter
II. 10 Translation by Richard Frye (1984), courtesy Beck
II. 14 Translation by David Potter
II. 35 a. Photo N. de Haan
        b. Photo J. C. N. Coulston
II. 36 Photo D. Mitchell
II. 37 Photo J. C. N. Coulston
II. 38 a–b. Photos O. Hekster
II. 39 a–b. Photos DAIR 70.993, 70.1000
II. 40 Photo T. Kaizer, courtesy A. Schmidt-Colinet
II. 41 Photo K. Oehrlein, courtesy Martin von Wagner Museum der
        Universität Würzburg, Leihgaben inventar ZA 111
II. 42 Courtesy E. Manders
II. 43 a. Courtesy British Museum London, BMC 273
        b. Courtesy CGB, r16.0248

Abbreviations

AE	*L'Année Epigraphique*
AncSoc	*Ancient Society*
ANRW	H. Temporini and W. Haasse (eds), *Aufstieg und Niedergang der römischen Welt* (Berlin 1973–)
BJ	*Bonner Jahrbücher*
BMCRE	H. Mattingly, *Coins of the Roman Empire in the British Museum* (London 1965–75)
CAH	*Cambridge Ancient History*
CIL	*Corpus Inscriptionum Latinarum*
CIS	*Corpus Inscriptionum Semiticarum*
CJ	*Codex Iustinianus*
CTh	*Codex Theodosianus*
Dig.	*Digest*
GRBS	*Greek, Roman and Byzantine Studies*
HSCP	*Harvard Studies in Classical Philology*
HTR	*Harvard Theological Review*
IG	*Inscriptiones Graecae*
ILS	H. Dessau, *Inscriptiones Latinae Selectae* (Berlin 1954–5^2)
JJP	*Journal of Juristic Papyrology*
JRA	*Journal of Roman Archaeology*
JRS	*Journal of Roman Studies*
LTUR	E. M. Steinby (ed.), *Lexicon Topographicum Urbis Romae* (Rome 1993–9)
Pan. Lat.	*Panegyrici Latini*
P.Diog.	P. Schubert, *Les archives de Marcus Lucretius Diogenes et textes apparentés* (Bonn 1990)
P.Dura	C. Bradford-Welles et al., *The Excavations at Dura-Europos: Final Report V.1. The Parchments and Papyri* (New Haven, CT, 1959)
P.Giss.	O. Eger et al., *Griechische Papyri im Museum des ober-*

hessischen Geschichtsvereins zu Giessen (Berlin and Leipzig 1910–12)

P.Oxy. B. P. Grenfell et al., *The Oxyrhynchus Papyri* (London 1898–)

P.Ryl. *Catalogue of the Greek and Latin Papyri in the John Rylands Library, Manchester 34 BAN*

P.Thmouis S. Kambitsis, *Le papyrus Thmouis 1, colonnes 68–160* (Paris 1985)

P.Yale *Yale Papyri in the Beinecke Rare Book and Manuscript Library*

PSI *Papiri greci e latini. Pubblicazioni della società italiana per la richerca dei papyri greci e latini in Egitto* (Florence 1912–)

RIC H. Mattingly and R. Sydenham (eds), *Roman Imperial Coinage* (London 1923–67)

RN *Revue Numismatique*

SEG *Supplementum Epigraphicum Graecum*

ZPE *Zeitschrift für Papyrologie und Epigraphik*

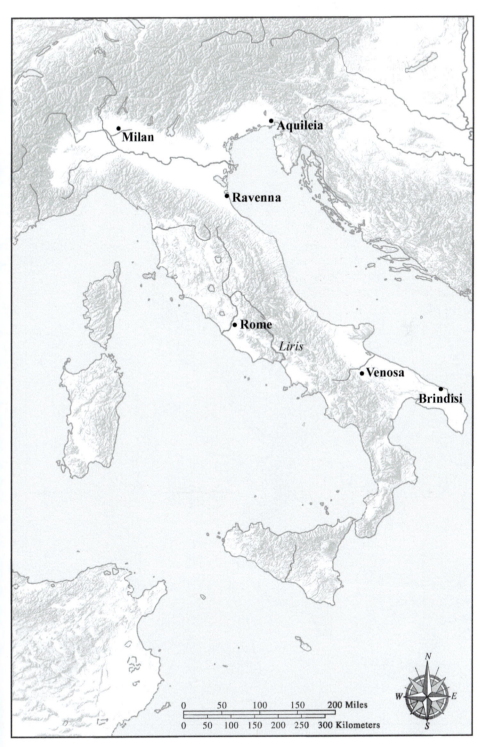

Map 1 Ancient Italy

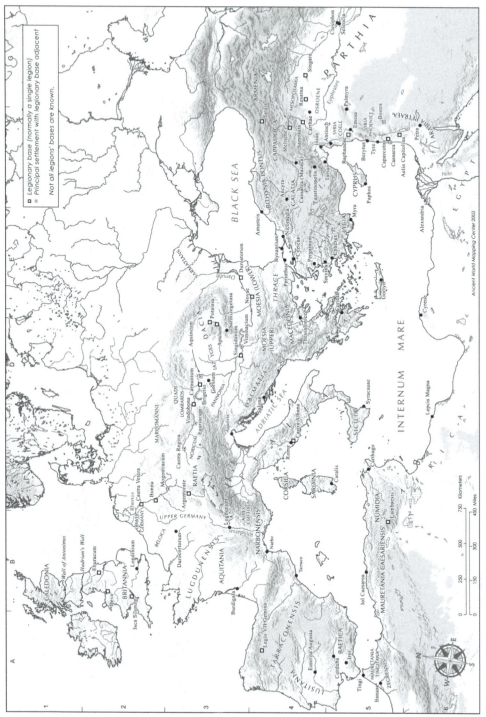

Map 2 Legionary bases in the Roman Empire (reign of Septimius Severus)

Legionary base (normally a single legion)
Principal settlement with legionary base adjacent

Not all legions' bases are known.

Ancient World Mapping Center 2003

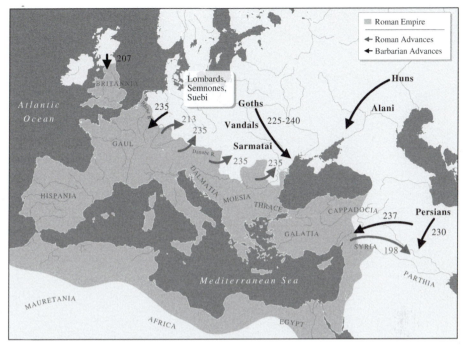

Map 3 Military advances from Septimius Severus to Gordian III

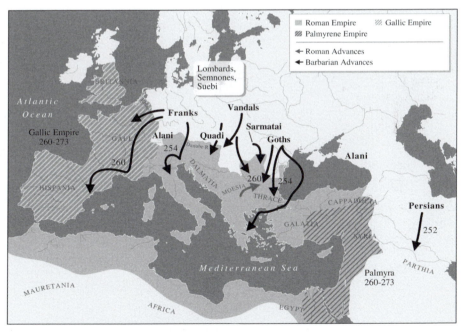

Map 4 Military advances from Papienus to Diocletian

Part I

Debates

INTRODUCTION

History and Narrative

When, on 1 January 193, the news started to spread through the city of Rome that the emperor Commodus had been assassinated the previous night, many senators must have been happy. Their relationship with the emperor had been problematic, and they will have hoped that any successor would take their interests more into consideration. They were wrong. The following century would limit senatorial influence beyond what could have been imagined. Almost twenty-five years after Commodus' death, in April 217, the first non-senatorial emperor was proclaimed (Marcus Opellius Macrinus), who reigned for fourteen months but never showed himself in Rome (**II 5 8.21**). Nearly twenty years later, the first professional soldier, a man of equestrian and not senatorial rank, became emperor (Maximinus Thrax, 235–8), again avoiding Rome throughout his reign (**II 5 9.1**). Another forty-five years passed before even the last gesture was abandoned. The emperor Carus (282–3) did not even ask for senators to acclaim him – his emperorship was based wholly on the support of his troops. The power to appoint emperors lay wholly with the soldiers, as was famously announced by the fourth-century author Aurelius Victor (**II 4 37**). Only shortly after did Diocletian (284–305) come to occupy the throne, and change the whole system of emperorship in the process. A new era had started.

Rome and its emperors

From 193 to 284 the Roman Empire knew over twenty-five more or less legitimate rulers, and an approximately equal number of usurpers who managed to take control of parts of the empire for at least some time. To say that there was a lack of dynastic stability is a massive under-statement. Still, some chronological demarcations are possible. First, there is the period up to 235. With the accession of Macrinus as an

3

aberration, the period was still dominated by dynastic tendencies. The death of Commodus was followed by a year of four emperors, much as had happened after Nero's suicide in 68. The ultimate victor of that struggle for power, Septimius Severus (193–211), founded a dynasty as Vespasian (69–79) had done before him. Even if the Severan dynasty consisted of a brother killing his brother (Caracalla, 211–17), a young transvestite presenting himself as the chief priest to a black stone (Elagabalus, 218–22), which was even depicted on coinage (**II 43 a, b; II 5 8.22**), and a fourteen-year-old boy who was dominated by his mother (Severus Alexander, 222–35), their claim to rule rested on descent from the Severan dynasty. In fact, those supporting the claims of Elagabalus (whose actual name was Varius Avitus Bassianus) in 218 even said that their candidate was Caracalla's bastard son, thus fabricating the closest possible link to the deceased emperor. This fake blood-line explains why Elagabalus is referred to as the 'false Antoninus' (**II 1 79.36**).

From 235 onwards, no single dynasty dominated Roman politics, though many rulers tried to establish one. Thus, there were as many as three Gordians. Unfortunately for them, the first two (who were father and son) were proclaimed emperor together and ruled for all of three weeks (238), whereas Gordian III (238–44) became emperor whilst thirteen years old. He died aged nineteen, possibly in battle after utter defeat, as is emphasised by the most important eastern source remaining, the great trilingual inscription of the neo-Persian ruler Shapur I at Naqsh-i-Rustam in Iran, in which he records the deeds achieved during his reign (**II 10 3–4; cf. II 36**) in Middle Persian, Parthian and Greek, so that all would be able to read the record of his greatness. Alternatively, Gordian died because of intrigues and army unrest. The latter is stated by Roman sources who all emphasise that Gordian obtained great success in war, but was 'betrayed by a companion', the later emperor Philip the Arab (244–9) (**II 9 13–20; II 5 9.2; II 4 27**) (Millar 2004: 162–3). More unfortunate even was Philip II, the son of Philip the Arab, who was appointed heir by his father six months after the latter gained the throne, and became joint Augustus before reaching the age of ten (247). It is hardly surprising that the son did not survive his father's death. Continuous attempts by emperors to have their sons rule with them only made ever more certain that an imperial son would not survive his father's fall from grace. An exception to the rule was the emperor Gallienus (253–68). He ruled longer without his father Valerian (253–60) than with him – notwithstanding the problems that arose when Valerian became the first ever Roman emperor to be captured in battle, eventually coming to a gruesome end, possibly having his body skinned as a trophy after years of humiliation (II 4 32; II 5 9.7; II 6 23; II 11 5.3–6).

During Gallienus' reign, problems seemed ubiquitous, leading to the onset of a Gallic counter-empire (260–74) – complete with emperors and usurpers – and a similar claim from Palmyra, with queen Zenobia a most infamous adversary (267–72). Gallienus was succeeded by a group of so-called 'Illyrian' emperors (268–82) (named after their general area of birth) who tried to impose order, with only limited success. Still, some problems were addressed by the emperor Aurelian (270–5), who once more unified the empire. Military men now ruled the realm. The Illyrian trend was broken by the emperor Carus (282–3) who, once again, attempted to establish a dynasty. It failed. Singularly unlucky to be struck by lightning (although some sources suggest his death was caused by illness, or simply by a man covering his tracks by setting Carus' tent on fire and blaming lightning), he was succeeded by his two sons Carinus and Numerian, both of whom seem to have died through betrayal and treason (Numerian's body was even carried around for several days in a closed litter, before the odour emanating from it made some soldiers wary enough to open it). Still, the constant claim to continuity by repeated attempts to found dynasties within a dynastically discontinuous chaos shows how certain habits die hard, even in the face of clear resistance. Eventually, the habit was broken by the commander of the imperial guard, Diocles, who took up power and, as Diocletian (284–305), insisted on many administrative and ideological innovations. According to some, he even changed the empire beyond recognition.

Politics and the provinces

Clearly, then, emperors found it problematic to control their realm. Internal struggles were only one reason for this. The situation was aggravated by pressure on the north and east borders of the empire. Changes among Germanic tribes around the end of the second century led to conflict and invasion across the Rhine and Danube, where tribes such as the Alamanni and Franks made life difficult for the Romans – even invading substantial parts of Gaul around 275 (**maps 3–4**). Towards the East, similar problems existed with invasions by the Quadi, Vandals, Sarmatai and Goths. Again, problems were not limited to the borders alone, with fighting taking place in the Balkans and on the coast of Asia Minor (**maps 3–4**).

On top of that, in 226 the Parthians lost control of their empire (consisting roughly of modern-day Iran, Iraq and Armenia and parts of Turkey, Georgia, Azerbaijan, Turkmenistan, Afghanistan and Tajikistan) to the so-called new Persians, reigned over by the Sassanid dynasty (**II 10 1–2**). All through Rome's history, the Parthians had been Rome's most feared enemy, the one real empire to exist beyond Rome. Continuous diplomacy and occasional border conflicts had, however, assured a fair measure of stability. Ironically, the fall of Rome's most feared enemy would lead to much more severe problems. The Parthians had ruled their empire as a sort of federation, with a large measure of autonomy for the diverse regions. The Sassanids were much more centralistic – and expansionistic. Their second ruler, Shapur I (240–72), would fight major campaigns on (the borders of) Roman territory from 252 to 264. Most of the time, the Persians were winning (**II 10 3–16**), most famously capturing Valerian in AD 260. In fact, the new Persian Empire would remain dominant for centuries, only ceasing to exist around the middle of the seventh century.

Clearly, the picture that arises is one of a century of upheaval. But that need not have had serious repercussions for all of the inhabitants of the empire as a whole. Certainly, people living in areas in which actual fighting took place would suffer, but throughout the third century there were zones in which the political and military unrest had remarkably few consequences (see below, Chapters 1 and 2). Yet even there, some indirect effects of the upheaval could affect daily life. The Antonine plague, which broke out in the Roman Empire towards the end of the second century, resurfaced again and again throughout the third century, and killed in places up to 20 per cent of the population. This, on top of further economic problems, led to changes in the structure of society (and the military) that had an impact beyond the areas in which depopulation took place (see below, Chapter 2).

In other areas, struggles between emperors and counter-emperors exacerbated the already precarious situation. Rampaging armies disrupted social and economic life, whether they were Roman or foreign armies, fighting each other or amongst themselves. Once normality was disrupted, it was often difficult to restore the balance – and impossible if soldiers were still (or again) roaming round (see below, Chapter 2). Some areas certainly suffered more from this than others. The period under discussion thus saw military and socio-economic disasters in some of the empire's territory, and even (temporary) fragmentation of its very geographic existence. At the same time, the empire also reached the height of its unification: the *Constitutio Antoniniana* (**II 20**; and see below, Chapter 3) of 212 granted Roman citizenship to almost all free inhabitants of the Roman Empire. Though this formed a culmination of earlier processes, it also brought with it important changes. The universalisation of Roman citizenship had implications for the status of Roman law. It also made the imperial cult a semi-state cult (see below, Chapter 4). After all, if all inhabitants were citizens, they all ought to participate in Roman cults, which included the imperial cult. The ruling emperor Caracalla even professed that uniting his people under the cult of Rome and the Roman gods would ensure *pax deorum*. That support of traditional Roman gods had been placed in doubt in both Rome and the provinces by the major religious changes which took place in the third century. The rise of Christianity may have been the most striking example, but it should be viewed alongside the development of other religious and philosophical schools, and continuing pagan ritual (see Chapter 5).

Historiography

Transitions tend to lead to discussion. Many people do not like change, and if change does occur, people want it to be to their advantage. In most situations, this is to the disadvantage of others. Inevitably, descriptions of events become highly biased, and sometimes politically laden. A change in dominance in socio-economic status can be a disaster or the final coming about of justice, depending on whose point of view is taken. On top of this, changes can be masked as continuity, whilst continuity can also be portrayed as change – depending on the purpose of the person presenting the picture. This makes it important to realise the point of view of the individuals producing texts and documents. Unfortunately, for the third century, this is often highly problematic.

For the ninety years or so between the death of Commodus and the accession of Diocletian a number of historical accounts by ancient authors exist. None of them gives a complete overview, nor is any of them particularly trustworthy. The beginning of the period is best catered for. The *Roman History* of the Bithynian senator Cassius Dio (II 1) (who lived from c. 163/4 till shortly after 229), which runs up to 229, is valuable, since the author witnessed many events himself, even being consul in 205/6 and then again, together with the emperor Severus Alexander, in 229. It is hardly surprising that his work is written with a senatorial bias. He also has a bias against soldiers (and emperors who boosted military interests too much), possibly because he was

forced out of Rome by the praetorian guard during his second
consulship. More problematic than the bias (which can after all be taken
into account) is the fact that almost all of the work was transmitted in
much abbreviated versions through eleventh- and twelfth-century
'highlights' (*epitomes*) by the Byzantine monks John Zonaras and
John Xiphilinus. Another contemporary history, by the non-senatorial
Herodian (c. 175–250), describes the period between 180 and 238 and
is transmitted whole. Herodian came from the East – possibly as a
freedman from Antioch – and was a minor official at Rome. His writing
is often anecdotal and not always reliable, since 'novelistic' choices
sometime ignore factuality (**II 2**). Still, as an eye-witness he can show us
at least how matters were seen at the time. Added to this, there is the so-
called *Historia Augusta* (also known as the *Scriptores Historiae Augustae*).
The work purports to be a multi-authored collection of biographies of
second- and third-century emperors (Hadrian to Numerian). It thus
gives an overview of all emperors and usurpers from the period under
discussion (**II 3**). But the work is notoriously unreliable and is used
sparingly here. Current consensus holds that the texts were written by a
single author in the late fourth century and that much of the content is
pure fiction, including invented documents, events and (probably) even
some of the usurpers. Still, the earlier 'lives' give some useful information, probably because the unknown author of the *Historia Augusta*
based himself on better original sources for the earlier period. On the
whole, anything that can be found solely in the *Historia Augusta* should
be used only with extreme caution. Where there is literary or archaeological backup, the *Historia Augusta* can be used to supply interesting
details. However, recent finds of coins by a usurper who had – until
these coins were found – been thought to be a fabrication of the *Historia
Augusta* show that one can also be overcautious. A certain Domitian
attempted to come to power, exactly as we were told (**II 48 c; II 3a 2.6;**
and see Chapter 4).

   For the period after 235, historians have mainly to rely on non-
contemporary texts, such as (apart from the *Historia Augusta*) the three
short chronological overviews by Aurelius Victor (*Book of the Caesars*;
31 BC–AD 360) (**II 4**), Eutropius (*Brevarium*; 753 BC–AD 364) (**II 5**)
and Festus (*Breviarium*; 753 BC–AD 364) (**II 6**). All worked in Roman
administration and published their books in the second half of the
fourth century. Of these, Eutropius is used here at length in order to give
a literary overview in the limited space available, whereas Victor and
Festus are used for complementary – or indeed contradictory – information. A similar abbreviated overview is the *Epitome de Caesaribus*, by

an unknown author. Much later still are the accounts by Byzantine authors such as the Syrian Zosimus (late fifth century) (**II 7**) or Zonaras (late eleventh century – mid-twelfth century), who both incorporate earlier sources in their histories of the world, such as the earlier mentioned *epitomes* of Cassius Dio, and the writings of the Athenian Dexippus, who wrote a history up to the death of Claudius II (AD 270). Dexippus was a member of an important Athenian family and participated in the politics of his time, which might explain why his life and views are known through various inscriptions and literary fragments (**II 12–13**). Alongside these texts other literary sources exist, with a wholly different kind of bias. These are what could be dubbed 'religious texts'; that is, written from a clear religious point of view, which can be historical, anecdotal or ritualistic. Prime amongst these are Christian writings, such as those of the Carthaginian bishop Cyprian (**II 29–30**), but also including interesting works like the *Book of Pontiffs*, which gives biographies of the first ninety bishops of Rome. In this category, one could also include prophetic books, of which the most influential are the notoriously opaque Sibylline Oracles. This corpus of texts consists of oracles predicting the future, written long after the event. The most important text for the period under discussion is the so-called Thirteenth Sibylline Oracle, which was assembled after Egypt was conquered by the Arabs in AD 646, but composed at various times in the actual periods it discusses. The main part (lines 89–154) was probably written in the summer of AD 253, the earlier lines before that. Its primary importance is that, with the great trilingual inscription of Shapur I, mentioned above, it is the only contemporary account covering the political events of the Roman Empire between AD 238 and the reign of Constantine (**II 9**; Potter 1990). Perhaps a more unexpected 'prophetic' work is the Bible – sections of which reflect ancient concerns, and can be an interesting historical source. Finally, much can be learned from legal texts, which can often be dated to individual reigns.

Material evidence is also an important source for the modern historian. Some of this can be textual, such as inscriptions and papyri. They can provide glimpses of life in other levels of societies, and on the periphery of empire. Funerary inscriptions, for instance, often show careers (*cursus honorum*) of individuals ignored by literary texts, such as soldiers or officials who did not quite make it to the top. Through papyri, wholly different sets of information have survived, ranging from private letters to wills (**II 19**; **II 23**) and important legal documents (**II 20**). Though at first sight these documents are much less biased than the literary ones, points of view and contexts must again be taken into consideration; people are unlikely to put career failures on funerary monuments, and not all wills and private letters are equally represen- tative. Furthermore, the 'epigraphic habit' of the third century was much less pronounced than in earlier periods (MacMullan 1982), which means that there are simply fewer inscriptions to work with.

Different kind of biases, often much less pronounced, must be taken into account when looking at non-literary texts. Archaeology allows us to reconstruct both public and private buildings, and can also give indications about the size (and fertility) of plots of agricultural land or the date when city walls were constructed. Unfortunately, the data that are produced are not always as straightforward as many historians believe, and are very much dependent on the starting point of the archaeologists. Other kinds of material sources, such as statues, reliefs or coins, have ideological purposes – which are not always self-evident. On top of that, it is not always clear who had these sources constructed. Again, caution must be used before reconstructing the Roman world from these sources with too much confidence.

All of this is not to say that a reconstruction of a history of Rome and its empire in the years from AD 193 to 284 is impossible. There are, however, many uncertainties, and much that is left open to debate. Not the least of these debates focuses on the relationship between the city of Rome and its provinces.

CHAPTER 1

A Capital and its Provinces

The Roman Empire, essentially, started as a city state growing out of proportion. This remained noticeable in the prime position in the empire of the city of Rome until at least the great reforms of Diocletian and his Tetrarchy (Rees 2004: 24–45). Up to the third century, however, Rome could have defended its position by pointing to the relative peace the Romans had brought. It is true, of course, that the first two centuries of imperial Roman rule had seen some rebellions, but the vast majority of these had been conflicts limited to restricted geographical areas (Pekáry 1987). Where rebellions had been more pronounced, few people (if any) had survived to tell the story. Rome did not suffer dissent lightly. Yet overall there had been little dissent, with provincial loyalty being the rule rather than the exception (Ando 2000). Equally importantly, Rome had managed to keep its frontiers safe, and from the reign of Augustus (31 BC–AD 14) onwards, it was a long time before any enemy forces marched on Roman soil. Whatever people may have thought of Roman rule (and life under Rome could be very brutal and unfair), this *pax Romana* must have been generally appreciated. This can be illustrated by a famous speech by Aelius Aristides (**II 8**), though one must remember that it was delivered in front of the emperor – which rarely leads to criticism.

Rome's prime position, as a result, was rarely challenged. Yet the certainty of Roman peace started to erode from the middle of the second century onwards. Marcus Aurelius (161–80) had to spend a substantial part of his reign at the frontiers, keeping different enemies at bay, in which he was severely hampered by the so-called Antonine plague, which started in the mid 160s and flared up again and again in the late second and early third century, in places taking the life of up to 20 per cent of the population (Duncan-Jones 1996: 116–17, 120–2). With fewer men to take up arms, his son and successor Commodus (180–92) chose to settle, rather than to fight. But even his attempts to keep the peace could not avoid widespread disturbances in the mid-180s in Britain, Gaul, Germany and Illirycum – going as far as the besieging of a Roman legion, the *legio* VIII Augusta, in AD 185 (Hekster 2002: 62–3). At the same time, however, peace in Spain, Africa and most of the East of the empire continued unabated. Central government still supported local cities in difficulties. When in need, the empire still turned to Rome.

The death of Commodus, and with it the end of the Antonine dynasty, temporarily upset peace in most of the empire, but did not shatter it. With no obvious successor, four aspirants aimed for the throne, Septimius Severus defeating his last competitor only in AD 197. One should never underestimate the disruption that civil war causes, and it had been 124 years since the last one, but there was every reason to believe that the victory of Severus would restore normality. Still, at the end of Severus' reign, he is alleged to have told his sons to take care of soldiers especially, and ignore everyone else. Those at least are the words of Dio, who lived at the time (**II 1 77.15.2**). Did this foreshadow the military bias of the soldier emperors? Likewise, it has been suggested that the reign of Severus marks the rise of the East. Towards the end of the second century, more new senators than ever came from the East (Halfmann 1979: 78–81), but that had not yet resulted in any emperor born east of the Adriatic. Septimius was born in Lepcis Magna (modern Libya), and never hid the fact (**II 5 8.18**). He had major building work undertaken in his town of origin, and emphasised its two patron deities, Melquart-Hercules and Liber-Bacchus, in many ways (*LTUR* 3, 25–6; *BMCRE* 5, 505–7; Scheid 1998: 16–17, 20–1). In fact, there have been notions of Septimius Severus as an 'African emperor'. These can be roughly separated into attempts to emancipate (Carlisle and Carlisle 1920; Jones 1972), which imply the importance of ethnic identity, and more historical ideas in which people from the same region are supposed to have known each other, and hence cooperated (Birley 1969). In any case, the debate on how 'African' Severus was, and how influential his 'African' friends, is, in the end, of only minor importance in comparison to the massive changes that the relationship between centre and periphery of the empire underwent in the third century.

A capital in trouble

In AD 193, the unthinkable happened for only the second time in Roman imperial history. The city of Rome was marched upon. At the time, four men claimed the throne (**II 1 74.14.3**): Didius Julianus in

Rome, and Septimius Severus, Clodius Albinus and Pesecennius Niger in various parts of the empire. Cassius Dio, who was present in Rome at the time, describes the defence measures taken by Didius Julianus, Septimius Severus' predecessor, with ridicule. Soldiers from the fleet were brought in for work they were not fit for, elephants that were supposed to carry heavy loads threw off their riders, and Julianus even strengthened the palace, so that he could lock himself in if everything went wrong (**II 1 74.16.1–4**). It is, of course, possible that this was how Julianus organised matters, but is more likely that here Dio betrays his bias. Julianus' behaviour as an emperor is described through a combination of commonplaces for bad rulers. Possibly he was a bad emperor, but Dio had also to portray him negatively to make Septimius' actions look good. Yet the main problem Dio had with Didius Julianus was the way in which the latter had come to power. In contravention of what Dio thought of as the grandeur of Rome, in 193 the emperorship was sold off by the praetorians, as if in an auction, and Julianus had been the buyer. The praetorians, who were the only soldiers present in Rome, simply decided to support the man who was going to pay them the most, a bidding war which Didius Julianus won (**II 1 74.11.2**). By making Julianus look bad, Dio made Severus' march on Rome understandable. But however justifiable some authors could portray Severus' reasons for marching on the capital to be, the fact is that for the first time since the start of the Flavian dynasty, Rome became a battlefield. Following the fighting in AD 69, there had been a conscious effort by those in power to re-establish the image of Roman supremacy, through emphasis on peace and stability, and the victories of the new dynasty (Hekster 2007: 97–8). Up to a point, Severus did the same, obtaining victories in the East in the years following his accession, and emphasising these (and his dynasty) in Rome through monuments and festivals. For instance, during the celebrations of the Secular Games in AD 204, Septimius and his sons took centre stage, as did, perhaps more surprisingly, the patron deities of Lepcis Magna (Scheid 1998: 16–17, 20–1). Perhaps this would have been sufficient, if their subsequent rule had been characterised by glorious peace. It was not.

To illustrate, one might take the point of view of an inhabitant of the city of Rome who lived up to the age of fifty. This was not an age that most third-century Romans could expect to reach, with a life expectancy at birth of about twenty, and of just under fifty for people at the age of ten. That is information which can be deduced from a list supplied by the jurist Ulpian, which gives multipliers to establish tax values of pensions – thus guesstimating probable life expectancy (Dig.

35.2.68 pr.; Frier 1982, 1999: 88). If our fictitious fifty-year-old had been
born in AD 150 and died in AD 200, his life would not have been without
disturbances. He would have been lucky to survive the Antonine plague,
which reached Rome in AD 166 and thrived in the city's urban crowds,
so that according to Dio sometime during Commodus' reign 'two
thousand persons often died in Rome in a single day' (Dio, 73.14.3),
translating as up to 300,000 deaths in total (Scheidel 2003: 171). Apart
from the eccentric behaviour of Commodus, life would otherwise have
been fairly tranquil, up until a massive fire in the city in AD 191, and the
march on Rome and civil war mentioned above following Commodus'
assassination, which would have lasted until just before the fictitious
Roman's death. A further characteristic would have been that in thirty-
four out of fifty years, the emperor would have been present at Rome,
often for protracted periods of time (Halfmann 1986: 210–23).

   Still, that life might have looked like a golden age for someone living
in Rome in the period AD 200–50. He would have seen two brothers,
both emperors, fight what came near to a civil war in the very city of
Rome itself (**II 2 4.4**; see also Chapter 4); a soldier becoming emperor
and not visiting the capital (AD 218); and the traditional supreme gods
of Rome being made subsidiary to a black conic stone (**II 43 a, b**). To top
it all, he would then have lived through a year of six different claimants
to the throne (AD 238), in which several magistrates, including the
urban prefect (*praefectus urbi*), were actually slain (**II 4 26**). The course
of events was extraordinary and is transmitted through Herodian
(7.5–7.10), Eutropius (**II 5 9.2**) and Aurelius Victor (**II 4 26–7**). In 238,
the elderly Gordian I was proclaimed emperor in Africa, though
Maximinus Thrax was still alive. The senate, however, declared him an
enemy of the state (*hostis*) and sided with Gordian. When rumours
arrived at Rome that Gordian had died, the senate was in difficulty, and
formed a committee of twenty advisors. After Gordian's death, with
Maximinus still alive, the senate chose two members of that committee,
Clodius Pupienus and Caelius Calvinus Balbinus (Aurelius' mentioning
'Caecilius' is a mistake), to become emperor. Though Maximinus was
killed shortly afterwards, making them sole emperors, their reign would
be brief. The military and the inhabitants of Rome much preferred
dynastic succession, and Gordian III, the young grandson of Gordian I,
was made Caesar. Within three months Pupienus and Balbinus were
killed by the praetorians, and Gordian III was sole ruler (Haegemans
2003). By that stage, Rome was also at war with Shapur, and Gordian
died following a calamitous Roman invasion in Mesopotamia. Only
the Thirteenth Sibylline Oracle (**II 9 7–20**) describes these events in

somewhat glorious terms, equating Gordian with the god of war. Even this oracular text, however, had to note how the fighting ended with Gordian's death, though, as mentioned above, the details are disputed (p. 4). His successor would perhaps have boosted spirits by the great festivities which marked Rome's millennium celebration in 248 (**II 5 9.3**), but even these were marred (and delayed) by the unrest in the realm at large. Our Roman would, in any case, have died just before new fighting broke out in Rome itself, with the pretender Valens Hostilianus trying (possibly on the insistence of the plebs) to claim the throne. In our man's lifetime, emperors would have been present in the capital in twenty-one out of fifty years, for stays which would be much shorter than before (Halfmann 1986: 221–36).

Applying the same system to AD 250–300, emperors would have been present for a total of eighteen out of fifty years, but most of these stays would have been extremely short ones in between campaigns (Halfmann 1986: 236–44). Disease would again strike Rome, the symptoms of which were particularly unpleasant (Cartwright 1972: 20–1). Hoping for divine support, coins were even minted for Apollo Salutarus – the old favourite god of Augustus, portrayed in his healing capacity. Whilst the outbreak of disease was in progress, Rome was marched upon again (AD 253), though fighting took place just north of the capital. In the end the reign of the victor Aemilian lasted only eighty-eight days, and was characterised by Eutropius in the most dismissive phrase possible (**II 5 9.6**).

The next eventful years were AD 259–60. In spring 260, the Persians captured Valerian (see pp. 4 and 6). This was a shocking event, described metaphorically in the Sibylline Oracle (**II 9 155–71**). In this confusing passage, the man 'show[ing] forth the number seventy' is Valerian. In Greek, his name started with the letter omicron, which was also the sign for that number. Similarly, the man 'of the third number' is Gallienus, whose name starts with gamma, the third letter of the Greek alphabet. The emperor is described as a bull, and the Persians, who famously used dragon banners, must then be the serpent (Potter 1990: 328–9). Shapur, for obvious reasons, was much more explicit, emphasising how the Roman emperor was taken prisoner (**II 10 10**). This event was outrageous, but did not take place in Rome. In the preceding winter, however, Germanic hordes (the tribes of the Semnoni and Juthungi) invaded Italy itself, taking thousands of captives. An inscription (**II 15**; and see below, p. 26) which was found at Augsburg mentions how Roman troops defeated these tribes on their return from the Italian peninsula, and freed the Italian prisoners. This important inscription forms material evidence that the situation was as bad as literary sources indicate (Bakker 1993). It should, however, be stressed that incursions into Roman territory happened more often, even if not in the heartland: in 177/8 Moorish invasions in Spain were met only by raising auxiliaries there, and a (probably) Severan inscription at Rhodes praises a man for the protection he supplied against pirates whilst *strategos* (official in charge of the area; Gordon et al. 1997: 226).

Ten years later, in the winter of AD 270/271, problems were again close to Roman experience when Alamanni and Jugurthi devastated northern Italy, causing the emperor Aurelian serious problems. Our imaginary Roman may have been distracted from this by fighting within the city itself. Aurelian's own official for the Roman mint, his *rationalis* Felicissimus, occupied the mint on the Caelian Hill and used it as a stronghold – possibly because he was held responsible for the ongoing debasement of coinage, or even for desecrating the emperor's image on the coins. After some fighting, Aurelian restored order, apparently with a vengeance. Eutropius' comment that the emperor's 'savagery' was necessary for the time shows how the situation in Rome had changed from the previous century (**II 5 9.14**; Bird 1994: 150). Even more momentous must have been the construction of the grand Aurelian wall (*LTUR* 3, 290–9; **II 35; II 7 1.49.2**). This new wall, construction of which started in 271, was 19 km long, and protected approximately three times the surface which was enclosed in the much earlier Republican walls. On the one hand, its construction showed the continued importance of Rome, now better protected than any other city in the empire; on the other hand, it showed the bankruptcy of the *pax Romana* in its traditional form. If Roman armies could no longer be trusted to guarantee even Rome's safety, why would people look to Rome for help, when help was needed? Carus' decision in AD 281 not even to ask for senatorial acclamation was insult added to Roman injury, but should not have been completely unexpected.

It is clear that life in Rome from AD 193 to AD 284 was rife with problems. However, it should be observed that this was the case in the city for most periods from the start of Roman imperial rule onwards. In fact, apart from the period AD 50–100, most fifty-year stretches saw civil unrest, exceptionally cruel rulers, disease and/or massive fires. This lends some weight to the famous statement by the great eighteenth-century historian of Rome, Edward Gibbon, that:

> If a man were called to fix the period in the history of the world, during which the condition of the human race was most happy and prosperous, he

would, without hesitation, name that which elapsed from the death of Domitian to the accession of Commodus. The vast extent of the Roman Empire was governed by absolute power, under the guidance of virtue and wisdom. ... A just but melancholy reflection imbittered, however, the noblest of human enjoyments. They must often have recollected the instability of a happiness which depended on the character of a single man. The fatal moment was perhaps approaching, when some licentious youth, or some jealous tyrant, would abuse, to the destruction, that absolute power, which they had exerted for the benefit of their people. (Gibbon 1776: I, ch. 3)

Even if this 'happy and prosperous' period would mainly have applied to the city of Rome (and not even there to all inhabitants), it is worthwhile to observe that though in the period under discussion life in Rome was visibly more unstable, it seems to have been stability that was the exception.

An empire at large

The problems in the capital are clear enough. Yet before the third century these had not led to problems in the relationship between capital and provinces. When looking at the problems that beset the Roman Empire in the third century, emphasis therefore needs also to be placed on the problems in the empire at large. These range from the embarrassing to the devastating, and vary wildly from region to region.

First, the embarrassing: this category entails problems such as brigandage, of which the actions of a man named Bulla Felix are the most apparent. This robber ravaged the Italian countryside for over two years, frustrating an emperor who had just left for Britain to put an end to the rebellion of barbarians there (Birley 1988: 168–70). Dio, who was a contemporary, describes the story at length (II 1 77.10). It is a wonderful account, with Bulla variously pretending to be a city's magistrate and a centurion, freeing his own men after they are captured and escaping authorities for a long time. Only through the help of a husband whose wife Bulla slept with was the latter tricked into capture. Yet in between the lines of the narrative, some points are striking. Bulla apparently led a group of several hundred men, and was sufficiently organised to trace movements around Rome, and the important Brindisi harbour (II 1 77.10.1–2; II 77.10.5; map 1). Also, it took personal action by the emperor to set matters right, after two years of disturbance in Rome's immediate hinterland (II 1 77.10.6). There had been brigandage before, occasionally even truly embarrassing moments like the one in which the hydraulic engineer of the third legion, Nonius

Datus, was confronted by brigands and stripped down to the waist (**II 16 8.2728**). The inscription in which this is described shows that the events happened in AD 152, when Datus was sent to the town of Saldae in Africa to solve a technical problem: workers had started digging a tunnel through a mountain from two different sides and had somehow failed to meet in the middle. These sorts of organisational problems, like brigandage, can be traced throughout Roman history, well before the third century. Brigandage, however, seems to have become truly widespread under Severus, who tried to put a stop to it, without proper results (Grünewald 2004).

Still, the situation was reasonably tranquil in several areas of the empire. The situation only becomes serious when problematic events accumulate within a certain region; the embarrassing in itself is only problematic when compounded by other upsets. In this respect, attention should be given to problems caused by military men, who, rather than easing the pressures of brigandage, seem to have caused problems themselves. For instance (**II 17**), at Ağa Bey Köyü, in Lydia (Asia) in the early or mid-third century, agents of the military police took nine inhabitants of this imperial estate hostage and released one of them only after receiving a substantial ransom. After turning to the procurators without result, the inhabitants addressed the emperor at Rome, either Septimius Severus or Philip the Arab, as had happened for centuries when there were problems. We do not know how the emperor reacted. It is, however, impressive to see that – even in the dire situation of the third century – the members of the estate were so organised that they could muster common resourses of some magnitude (Hauken 1998: 46–7). Similar problems arose in the town of Skaptopara (in modern Bulgaria), during the reign of Gordian III (**II 16 3.12336**). Here, soldiers, private visitors, and even the procurators and governors with their staff confiscated goods and demanded accommodation, all without payment. This is related to the more general notion of *angareia* or *vehiculatio*, a system which obliged provincial subjects to provide transport and lodging for official Roman travellers based in the provinces. This system was problematic enough in itself, but Skaptopara was apparently so attractive, with its spa-like water, that 'official' guests from afar came to the town, and demanded hospitality. Again, people turned to local authorities, in this case the governor, who forbade the military agents to continue the abuses, but without result. As in Ağa Bey Köyü, the town sought help from the emperor to end this hopeless situation. As this petition from 20 December 238, however, makes clear, the emperor sent the townspeople straight back to the governors

(Hauken 1998: 98, 117). However awkward the situation was, the emperor was not getting involved.

Secondly, there were devastating problems, demonstrated clearly by fighting at frontiers (**maps 3–4**). Here, the differences from earlier periods are more pronounced. Most striking are the major frontier problems up to and including the capture of Valerian – by most definitions a momentous occasion, unsurprisingly mentioned by a barrage of sources (see above, pp. 4, 15; **II 4 32; II 5 9.9; II 6 23; II 11 5.3–6**). When set in rough chronological order the list of major military engagements is startling: in AD 209, Septimius Severus fought the Caledonians in Britain, who had rebelled in AD 207 (**map 3; II 1 77.15.2**), whilst in AD 213 Caracalla defeated invading Cenni and Alamanni, later to invade Parthia (AD 216). Ten years later, the Sassanid dynasty took over in the East, and started to reconquer territory from Rome. From the 230s onwards, the Alamanni raided the area on the Rhine, Dacians and Thracians started fighting along the Danube, and Mesopotamia fell to the Sassanids (AD 237). A Gothic invasion in Moesia was repelled. The 240s were dominated by fighting between Romans and Persians, with changing fortunes. In 243 the battle of Resaina in northern Mesopotamia was a great Roman success for Gordian III and his father-in-law, the praetorian prefect (*praefectus praetorio*) Timesitheus (**map 4**). That success, however, was greatly diminished by the Persian victory at Fallujah on the Euphrates a year later, and Gordian's death (above, pp. 4, 15). Philip the Arab even ended up signing a treaty with Shapur.

The extended section on Philip in the Sibylline Oracle (**II 9 21–34**) wrongly states that Philip comes from Syria and – as nearly always in the oracles – identifies him by the numerical value of the first letter of his name. Both the office starting with the first letter (a = augustus) and the twentieth (k = Caesar) will be filled by a name which starts with the equivalent of five hundred (ph = Philip) (see above, p. 15; Potter 1990: 219). The treaty which Philip and Shapur made in AD 244 is also mentioned, as an oath between the wolves (the Persians) and the dogs (Philip and his son) who are the guardians of the flock (the inhabitants of the Roman Empire). The treaty is similarly mentioned by Shapur (**II 10 4**), who in his account of all campaigns continuously stresses the enormous losses of the Romans, both in terms of manpower (**II 10 4, 9**) and in terms of cities and areas that were captured and destroyed (**II 10 5–9, 11–15**). The names mentioned in the inscription have been used to reconstruct the various campaigns between the Romans and Persians, but more than anything else they show the immensity of the area that was affected by the fighting between these two superpowers. Shapur gives details of the treaty, stating that that Rome paid 500,000 gold coins (*aurei*) and became tributary to the Persians. It seems clear that Shapur deemed Philip to be in his debt from an important rock relief at Bishapur, just south of the modern town Faliyan in Iran (**II 36**). The relief is somewhat damaged, since a stone aqueduct was built along the rock, but the image is still recognisable. It shows the great victories of Shapur I (seated on a horse) against Rome. Trampled under the horse's legs lies Gordian III, whom Shapur claims he killed. Standing behind the Persian king, held by him, is the captured emperor Valerian (see above, p. 15). The third Roman emperor depicted in this relief is Philip. He is kneeling in front of the king's horse, showing his allegiance. Similar friezes were carved elsewhere in Persian territory. That need not mean that all which Shapur proclaims in his victory inscriptions and reliefs is wholly true. It was in his interest to show himself in the best possible ways, ignoring any possible setbacks. Still, it cannot be doubted that the Sassanid Empire was making life very difficult for Rome.

At the same time, trouble along the Danube continued, something that is again emphasised in the Sibylline Oracle (**II 9 35–49**). Rome (the Roman Ares) is at war with German tribes and will win, whilst simultaneous war will not bring victory to the Persians. In fact, the oracle proclaims, the Persian shall not obtain victory as long as Rome holds on to Egypt, the nurse of the Italians at the Nile, supplying Rome with grain. As it was, fighting with Goths and Germans seemed finally to quieten down in AD 248/9 (partly through an important victory by the emperor Decius), only to flare up again in the 250s (**map 4**), when Goths crossed the Danube, and ended up killing Decius at the battle of Abrittus in AD 251. This was the first time a Roman emperor was killed fighting barbarians and it must have been noted throughout the empire (**II 9, 100–2**). Still, Eutropius (**II 5 9.4**) simply states that Decius and his son were killed in barbarian territory, omitting to state whether they were killed in battle or through treachery. Now trouble really started. In AD 252 the Persians under Shapur I attacked. In 254 the Goths under their king Kniva followed. Within a few years Syria and Armenia (to the east of modern Turkey) were overrun, Thrace was sacked and even Pannonia, just northeast of the Italian peninsula, was devastated (**map 4**).

Sources are universal about the dreadfulness of the reigns of Gallus and Volusianus (described as the bastard son in the Thirteenth Sibylline Oracle). Plague and famine worsened a situation already going wrong (**II 9 103–12; II 5 9.5**). This in turn was exacerbated by Frankish invasions into Germania Inferior, Gaul and Spain from 254 to 261. Forts along the Lower Rhine were destroyed – including the stone fortress of Gelduba, whose whole cohort, the *cohors II Varcianorum equitata*, was annihilated. A mass grave, probably with the soldiers' bodies, has been excavated in a temple of Mithras. Of the important towns, only Colonia Agrippina survives (Eck 2007: 36–7). In AD 260, the Franks even managed to invade northern Italy (**II 5 9.7–9.8**), following the Alamannic example of AD 258, and reached the town of Ravenna (**map 1**). In the same years, the Goths ravaged Asia Minor and Juthungi crossed the upper Danube. Finally, and most shockingly in Roman eyes, in AD 260, after some years of reasonable peace in the East, the eastern part of the Roman armies – weakened by plague – were obliterated at Edessa by Shapur's troops. Valerian – as mentioned above – was captured, according to Shapur alongside many generals and senators, and the Roman armies were destroyed (**II 10 9–11**). This moment is often, and perhaps rightly, described as the low point of the Roman Empire. Rome seemed a byword for instability, rather than the peace it had guaranteed for centuries (**II 5 9.7; II 5 9.8**). To this new situation, different regions reacted in different ways.

Reactions to Rome

Of course in many areas people kept looking for help from Rome, and notwithstanding the difficulties, the Roman military was very often successful. But in other areas, people took their own initiatives. Just a few years after the capture of Valerian, in AD 267/8, Goths and Heruli invaded and overran large parts of Greece. They are said to have come with over 300,000 men on 6,000 ships (Zosimus 1.42–3; **II 3a 13.6–8**) and, whatever their true number, certainly caused massive devastations in Thessaly and Greece – as the archaeological record makes clear. For instance, at Olympia, a defence wall was created surrounding the main temple to Zeus, in which the most valuable statues were collected. Likewise, in Athens a last line of defence was created (the Valerian wall) which included only a small area north of the Acropolis (Millar 2004: 293). In these dire circumstances, the historian P. Herennius Dexippus (above, p. 9) excelled as general and repelled the barbarians – knowing that the imperial fleet was coming to help, and encouraging his men through emphasis on the Athenian patriotism of old. From the posts and functions which are recorded on the most important inscription connected with him, Dexippus was clearly a member of an important Athenian family (**II 13**). The most senior position he had held was the archonship, but he is also praised as a writer of the history of his own age. Important to note is the absence of any Roman offices. Dexippus and his family could well have sought office at Rome, but must have decided to remain at Athens and focus on their position there (Millar 2004: 283). In his own account of the event, Dexippus describes his rallying speech at some length and, unsurprisingly, emphasises its importance in hardening the minds of men (**II 12**). The speech stresses the locality of the fighting. Not only are the Athenians in an advantageous position because they hold the high ground, they also have more to lose, and will therefore fight more bravely than their enemy. The emperor's fleet is mentioned so as to emphasise that the situation is not hopeless, but greater emphasis by far is on the glory, not just for the individual, but also the city, and indeed the whole of Greece. Fighting for the freedom of Greece is a role the Athenians have inherited from their forebears, or so Dexippus claims. The enemies of the Roman Empire, in this instance, became enemies of Athens, who were to be repelled by Athenians, led by a local man, defending local history and honour.

There are other examples of civilian resistance to the unrest, mostly through rapid construction of walls enclosing limited parts of cities, but occasionally also through actual force – as indicated by inscriptions celebrating the repelling of enemies (*AE* 1928. 38; Millar 2004: 296). This process is not always straightforward. For instance, when Shapur I was attacking the Roman Empire for the third time in the 250s, his advance was stopped short when 'rustic slingers' from the neighbourhood managed to defeat his army. Had Roman troops arrived in time and managed to defeat Shapur's troops themselves, the local slingers might well have been described as brigands. In this case, however, the rustic slingers carried the day. They were called upon by the local priest Sampsigeramus, who has been identified with the usurper Uranius Antoninus (Malalas XII; Rubin 1995: 134–5). A locally important person managed to rally the troops and inflict defeat upon the enemy; he then made an even bolder demand. It could even be argued that sometimes the claim for the throne was necessary to obtain the prestige that was necessary to order people around and defeat the enemy.

There was, in any case, always the risk that local 'saviours' would set their sights too high. Indeed, many of the usurpers were generals who had been unusually successful. The prestige gained by great victories – especially in a period when great victories were no longer the rule – could catapult generals into (near) power. That risk in itself was not new. It may have been fear of a victor's prestige which caused Nero to order the great general Corbulo's suicide in AD 66 (Griffin 1984: 117). More recently, Marcus Aurelius had been confronted by a confusing rebellion by his erstwhile confidant Avidius Cassius, whose military powers had been substantial (Hekster 2002: 34–7). What was new, however, was the prolonged disturbances in many different areas of the empire simultaneously – and the fact that central authority could no longer prevent problems, even if it often could solve them. For some regions, local 'saviours' became the first point of reference, and it would only be a question of time before these 'saviours' became the people to adhere to.

In two cases, however, the next obvious step – claims to the supremacy in the empire as a whole – was never taken, since the 'usurper' claimed supremacy only in a more limited area. To be precise, following Valerian's capture two parts of the empire claimed autonomy from, but no authority over, Rome.

Peripheral centres

In the first half of the third century, certain parts of Roman territory suffered more unrest than others. The eastern frontier, increasingly pressed by the Sassanids, was clearly one of the areas suffering more. In such troubles, the rich and somewhat peripheral caravan city of Palmyra in Syria (**map 4**) was of importance to Rome, all the more after the capture of Valerian. The importance was increased further through clever manoeuvring by the Palmyrene Septimius Odaenathus, who had become senator, occupying some formal position at Palmyra, possibly even becoming the magistrate in command of the province (*legatus*) of Syria Phoenice (Potter 1990: 380–94; Millar 1993: 165) and who both helped Gallienus fight Shapur (apparently recovering Mesopotamia) and killed the usurper Quietus. After Shapur's victory over Valerian, the Persian troops wreaked havoc on Syria, Cilicia and Cappadocia (**II 10 11**). In doing so, Shapur divided his army. This is clear from the fact that the cities mentioned in Shapur's *Res Gestae* (**II 10 12–15**) cannot have been taken by a single army in the stated sequence, whilst at the same time, areas in the *Res Gestae* are named in the order in which they were taken. From the organisation of the cities in the inscription, David Potter has rightly argued that Shapur split up his main force into three sections (Potter 1990: 338–40). These sections then ran into trouble against Roman 'counter-measures', which are mentioned in the Thirteenth Sibylline Oracle. One of these was led by Macrianus, who is described as a 'well-horned hungry stag in the mountains', which probably implies that he kept to the hills (II 9 155–71). Perhaps more important even, a naval officer named Callistus (the bow-footed goat) seems to have managed to seize Shapur's gold and harem. Both of them, however, as well as the Persian 'venom-spitting' beasts, are destroyed by the 'sun-sent, dreadful, fearful lion, breathing much fire', Odaenathus (II 6 23; II 5 9.10).

The latter's position following this victory is the matter of fierce debate, with different sources (and different modern authors) claiming different things. Later (but unreliable) sources state that Odaenathus received either emperorship or general command over the East. But Palmyra remained a Roman colony (*colonia*) and there is no real evidence for secession in the 260s. Although near-contemporary inscriptions call Odaenathus 'restorer of the whole east' (on a statue base from a colonnade at Palmyra; II 14 2.3946) or even 'king of kings' (on a milestone of Vaballathus; II 14 2.3971), which was later reused under Diocletian, the evidence is posthumous, when Palmyra had certainly changed course (Millar 1993: 170). It seems that, though he was *de facto* ruler of the East, Odeaenathus stressed his allegiance to Rome. Gallienus may have held little actual control in Palmyra and its wider surroundings, but Rome could still claim to be its emperor. This changed after Odaenathus' murder in AD 267/8, with the ensuing advancement of his second wife Zenobia and their son Vaballathus. They too may have temporarily accepted Roman supremacy, but the problematic status quo seems only to have been possible for a person with Odeaenathus' prestige and accomplishments. To make this claim hereditary – and even place power in the hands of a woman – was unacceptable to Rome, as is still reflected in the much later *Historia Augusta* and in Festus' text, though much less so in the account by Zosimus, which is an important source for the whole affair (II 3a 13.1–5; II 6 24; II 7). The *Historia Augusta* stresses how Zenobia had the strength and cunning of a man and outclassed many emperors in an unwomanly way, making some detrimental remarks about Gallienus on the way.

Lest the power of this 'Palmyrene Empire' be underestimated, their forces, as Zosimus states, entered neighbouring Roman provinces (II 7 1.44.1, 1.50.1). In Arabia, a milestone celebrates *Imperator Caesar Lucius Iulius Aurelius Septimius Vaballathus Athenedorus, Persicus Maximus, Arabicus Maximus, Adiabenicus Maximus, Pius Felix Augustus* (*ILS*, no. 8924). Zosimus is also right in claiming that Palmyrene influence, though somewhat convoluted, stretched all the way to Egypt, since Vaballathus and Aurelian were jointly acclaimed there (Rea 1972: 16). A coin minted at Antioch in AD 271 depicting Vaballathus on the obverse and Aurelian on the reverse shows power relations in that important city (**II 48 b**). What had started as a helpful reaction against a threat to Roman rule had become a threat to that very rule itself. Authority had become too obviously fluid, and Aurelian, who in many ways would temporarily restore order in the empire, in AD 272 mounted a campaign against what had only recently been an integral part of the empire (Watson 1999: 70–5). Again, Zosimus' account is illuminating. It shows (**II 7 1.49–1.50**) quite how difficult the beginning of Aurelian's reign was, with problems near Italy as well as further afield. It also emphasises nicely the precarious balance between Rome and the Persians. When Zenobia is losing heavily her solution is to cross the Euphrates, which was the furthest limit of Roman power, to ask the Persians for help (**II 7 1.55.1–2**). Zosimus may be right in stating that it was Zenobia's escape that worried Aurelian, but he may well have been more uncomfortable about a possible new fight with the Persians. In the end, Rome won, re-establishing supremacy. But the necessity of doing so was telling.

Nor was the eastern unrest without consequences. Take the city of Apamea in Syria; fully rebuilt after an earthquake in AD 115 had destroyed it, with exceptionally long colonnades (Balty 1988: 91), it was the home of over 100,000 inhabitants, including the future emperor Elagabalus' father. The Persian wars made it an important Roman military base – and even the winter headquarters of the *legio* II Parthica. The many military inscriptions found in consequence make the Museum of Apamea one of the world's foremost places for the study of third-century legionary activities (Balty 1988: 99). Different units were encamped at Apamea at one moment or another, as a result of the third-century troubles: the *legiones* XIII and XIV Gemina, III Gallica, IV Scythia and IV Flavia; the XIV *cohors urbana* and possibly the *ala I Flavia Augusta Britannica* and *ala I Ulpia Contariorum* (Balty 1988: 102). These different units were to bring people from many different origins together in one town. But records of this city life suddenly end with Shapur's invasion and taking of the town in AD 252. Though Apamea was later to become the home of a famous Neoplatonist school, and though Amelius Gentilianus from Etruria, who was Plotinus' pupil, settled there in AD 269, the days of military activity had suddenly ended. Life would never be the same again.

Still, the 'Palmyrene Empire' had long accepted Roman sovereignty. The same cannot be said for the 'Gallic Empire' which formed an autonomous area within Roman territory for almost fifteen years (AD 260–74). Again, as with Odaenathus, it was a military commander under Roman authority who both solved and caused problems at local level, in this case Marcus Cassianus Latianius Postumus, Gallienus' commander on the Rhine. He rebelled against Gallienus' son Saloninus – allegedly because the latter had claimed for himself the booty of a battle which Postumus had distributed amongst the soldiers. Soldiers rebelled, and Postumus was proclaimed emperor. Cologne was marched upon, and in the end the city handed over Saloninus, who was put to death (**II 4 33; II 5 9.9;** Zosimus 1.38.2; Zonaras 12.24.10–12). It has been often thought that in fact the direct cause of this usurpation was the defeat of Valerian in 260. In this view, the humiliation of Rome caused Postumus to take up arms. In 1992, however, as mentioned above, an important epigraphic find at Augsburg, dated 11 September 260, provided new evidence (**II 15**). Erected by the otherwise unknown Marcus Simplicinius Genialis, it is a dedication to *Victoria* for her aid in destroying the Semnoni and Juthungi. These, as mentioned, were the Germanic hordes who invaded Italy, taking many captives. On invading the territory which Postumus was in charge of they were defeated, enabling the commander to become a local saviour – taking up the name *Germanicus maximus* in the process (Drinkwater 1987: 26, 89; Jehne 1996). This might be the very battle about which the discussion of booty arose, but is, in any case, yet another example of a locality looking to its own for protection, rather than to Rome. It is, therefore, more than coincidental that later sources praise Postumus for the fact that he rescued Gaul when almost the whole empire was lost (**II 5 9.9**). It was his local military pre-eminence which gave him a power base.

Unlike other usurpers, however, and for reasons that cannot be retraced, Postumus recognised the limits of his power base, and refused to march on Rome. Thus, he was able to become the 'defender of the West', and create a Gallic Empire which survived his death. He even organised his territory as a miniature Rome, using Roman titulature, and minting coins which were recognisably Roman. These coins did, however, include local legends, emphasising for instance Gallic epithets of the demi-god Hercules, like 'Deusoniensi' (**II 48 d**). Still, this was never going to be an acceptable situation for the ruler at Rome, and Gallienus tried to remedy the problem. He failed, but after Aurelian managed to restore order in the East, the West was his inevitable next point of attention. In the summer of AD 274 he defeated Tetricus, the last ruler of the Gallic Empire, and his son. In a triumph, Aurelian made Zenobia and Tetricus walk before his chariot, depicting his victory (**II 5 9.13; II 6 24**). The fact that this moment is included in both Eutropius' and Festus' brief summaries of Aurelian's reign may well show the impact that this triumph had on contemporaries. The empire was whole again.

Rome's decentralisation

Under the emperor Aurelian, whose name has already surfaced several times, unity was finally restored for a certain measure of time. His immediate successors, with some success, tried to keep this relative order, although the list of more or less legitimate emperors in the period under discussion shows in how much chaos the Roman political system still was. Together, the rulers from 268 to 282 are called the 'Illyrian' emperors, from their general area of birth (**II 4 39**). These were new kinds of emperor, with different backgrounds from what had until not too long before been the standard. This is clear from the emphasis by the sources on the consular background of the emperor Tacitus, who was made emperor in 275 (**II 4 36; II 5 9.16**). As it happened, proclaiming the seventy-five-year-old Tacitus may have not been a clever move, but it is his status as consul which Aurelius Victor emphasises. Tacitus, by this account, was Rome's attempt to reclaim the right to appoint emperors from the soldiers; that he was killed only a few months later showed that Rome was no longer in charge. The fact that holding consular status had become the exception for an emperor shows how much had changed in this respect since Macrinus' emperorship. Even Victor had to accept (**II 4 39**) that in dire times dire men were needed to rule well. It is, in fact, telling that the notion that the senate chose Tacitus for his status seems to have been an invention of Victor (Syme 1971: 238). Rome's position in electing emperors had long gone.

A similar development can be seen within the armies. Being Roman (or indeed from the Italian peninsula) had long become the exception, with a massive differentiation of backgrounds the new norm. The need for more soldiers had broadened the recruiting area, with ever more men in the armies, as a letter from a certain Isis to her mother Termuthion makes clear. In this Egyptian papyrus, Isis, who has apparently just travelled from a small Egyptian town to the great city of Alexandria, salutes many members of her family, and ends by stating that there is no reason why Aio (who must be somehow related to her) should not join the army – since everybody seems to go there (**II 18**). In fact, Rome has started to look outside the empire for possible troops, recruiting men from beyond the frontier. This has been described as the 'barbarisation of the army' (Speidel 1975: 203). Still, notwithstanding the background of soldiers, the military language was Latin, as is testified by, amongst other inscriptions, early third-century inscribed Latin poems from two non-Latin centurions in the military outpost of Bu Njem in the Tripolitania Desert (Adams 1999). All the same, the difficulties in recruiting soldiers, and in keeping them happy, are also obvious from the enormous pay rises in the third century, first a 50 per cent rise under Caracalla, and then a staggering doubling of pay under Maximinus Thrax in 235 (Speidel 1992: 106).

Both these developments will be discussed in more detail in later chapters; for now it is important to realise that at all levels, the dominant place of the city of Rome was disappearing. The emperor was no longer from Rome, nor did he reside in the city. Without a clear dynasty in Rome and without assured Roman-ness in the military, the centrality of Rome and the permanence of the Roman Empire were no longer a given. This changing attitude can be clearly traced in the sources. Before the third century, there were no clear words indicating the fortified boundaries of the Roman Empire. There was the notion that soldiers based at the frontier made the empire secure, but this was mainly to stress that the soldiers were not in the cities. Indeed, Aristides in his famous address on Rome (**II 8**) emphasised that fortresses did not need soldiers. In this way he stressed how well Rome controlled the cities within its empire. There was no discussion about a threat from without. The notion of a *limes*, which in modern literature has come to 'indicate permanent defensive structures or formal military and administrative organization' (Isaac 1988: 130), became possible only after the many defensive wars in the third century. In fact, in the middle of such defensive wars, the Thirteenth Sibylline Oracle explicitly equates the borders of the empire with the walls of Rome (**II 9 103–12**). Before these defensive types of wars, also, dedications on behalf of the safety of the whole Roman Empire were unheard of. In the third century, there are inscriptions which testify to existing fears for the continuation of the empire as a whole. One is on an altar from Gressenich (near Aachen) and can be dated to AD 238. The altar is dedicated not to the safety of the ruling emperors, as is standard, but for the entire Roman Empire (**II 16 13.7844**; Eck 2007: 33–4; cf. *AE* 1965.30).

This changing awareness had implications for the city of Rome. Its centrality was still clear for Aelius Aristides (**II 8**). But the reforms of the Tetrarchy would allow for four rulers of the empire, none of whom ruled from Rome. The practicalities of keeping the frontiers in order meant that Rome lost its automatic primacy. This did not happen overnight, nor was Rome's abandonment formally accepted. A panegyric delivered in 289 explicitly expects the emperors to go back to

Rome once their work on the frontiers is completed. In doing so, however, the author admits that Rome at that time was deserted (*Pan. Lat.* 10(2).13–14). Likewise, a triumphal arch for the emperor Galerius has a telling panel on the east face of the south pier, in which the goddess Roma is still depicted as a personification of the realm but the city of Rome is no longer one of the four major cities of the empire, which are depicted behind the goddess (**II 37**). After the third century, the goddess Roma was only rarely depicted on coins, and the she-wolf who nursed Romulus and Remus almost disappeared from imperial iconography (Hekster 1999: 722). Still, Rome remained of at least symbolic importance. Under the Tetrarchy, it was no imperial residence, but still the extraordinarily large baths of Diocletian were constructed. Also, as late as 306 the usurper Maxentius could use Roman discontent about the lessened importance of the city to bid for the empire for a substantial period of time, by basing himself in Rome, and emphasising its primacy in the empire (Hekster 1999: 724–37). Finally, as we shall see later (see below, Chapter 3), the weakened position of Rome did not mean a weakening of the sense of being Roman, or of the importance of being Roman. It is telling that even Postumus organised his Gallic Empire in Roman terms, and used Roman institutions.

At the beginning of this chapter, the question was put whether Septimius Severus' reign foreshadowed the rise of the east (or in more general terms, the periphery) and his famous last words (**II 1 77.15.2**) the rise of the military. Both of these developments will recur in later chapters. Still, it must already be clear that the answer cannot be straightforward. Severus won his victory with the aid of the eastern legions, and the continuous warfare at Rome's eastern frontier would add to those legions' importance (Millar 1981: 221–39). Yet earlier emperors had won their victory from the East, and the continuous and often calamitous events that occurred in the third century are hardly connected with Severus' rule. Furthermore, the debate on Severus as 'African' emperor may be of little importance, but it is essential to note that emperors had their networks, and just as Severus used his 'African' connection, so third-century emperors would promote the men with whom they were surrounded, and whom they trusted. This, combined with continuous fighting at the borders, meant that – as we shall see in the next chapter – military men from frontier zones gained prominence, which limited in practice the importance of members of the traditional families from Rome. Also, the position of Rome changed with the rise of local 'heroes', who were essential in defending the empire, but also showed that the *pax Romana* was no longer guaranteed by the city of Rome. There had been local heroes before the third century, and also troubles in the heartland, fighting at the borders, and emperors who came to power from outside the Italian peninsula. As will be clear throughout this book, there are precedents for almost every individual event which together constitute third-century history. The culmination of all of these events, however, would transform Rome and its empire. Continuity could always be stressed, and was often stressed by the powers that be. But people throughout the empire must have become aware that there was now a continuous period of near-exception in at least some parts of the Roman world. Not the least of these had to do with the increasing importance of the armies for administration and for developments in the economic framework of the empire.

CHAPTER 2

Economy, Armies and Administration

Increase in warfare, problems at the frontiers, empire-wide epidemics, and a great many emperors in a relatively short period of time: it is unsurprising that this situation was to have profound effects on Roman society in many parts of daily life. First, of course, there were economic consequences. One can trample land only so often, and lose only so many men to work it, before plots begin to be laid bare. In a society which is overwhelmingly rural, that is a serious problem. Second, this economic effect was strongly linked to the armies. Who, after all, did most of the trampling, and requisitioned food? The link between armies and economics was also strong since paying the soldiers was the single most expensive financial obligation of the Roman state – in practice of the emperor. Third, the changed situation had repercussions for the way the empire was run administratively, again with an increased role for military men, whose experience was becoming increasingly important. All three effects are much discussed in ancient and modern sources.

Economic disturbance and geographic differentiation

Many discussions on the economic situation of and changes in the period from AD 193 to 284 start with a famous treatise by the Christian Cyprian of Carthage (born c. AD 200), who was bishop of Carthage from 248 till his death as a martyr in AD 258/9: the address *To Demetrianus* (**II 29**). In it, he tries to refute the claim that the Christians were responsible for the economic devastations of his time, at the same time naming the economic (and other) problems people had to live with (**II 29 3**). The picture he paints is very bleak. The world has grown old; seasons have changed to man's disadvantage, resources have grown fewer. Furthermore (**II 29 5**), wars and illnesses are ever more common.

31

Yet this is simply the pattern of life, Cyprian argues (**II 29 3**). Everything diminishes when it grows old, men as much as knowledge or discipline. This, he continues, has always been the way of the world, and it would be wrong to blame the Christians (**II 29 4**). The trustworthiness of Cyprian as a source has often been discussed, with contradictory conclusions. He clearly related the events he witnessed as a foreshadowing of Judgement Day. For instance, the increase of warfare and plagues is directly linked to divine action; evils will multiply in the last days of mankind, for God demands his worship (**II 29 5**). This mode of viewing the world can either mean that Cyprian started from what he saw and related that to his religious notions (so the events were there), or that what he saw was coloured or even inspired by his religious notions, such as apocalyptic commonplaces (so the events may not have been quite so bad) (Alföldy 1973; Strobel 1993). The climatological changes which Cyprian mentions cannot, in any case, be confirmed by 'scientific' data. A recent attempt to trace solid evidence for environmental changes in the third century found that the data were difficult to date exactly. Through what could be dated, however, it seemed rather that Europe was already getting colder and wetter in the second century. The environment may have aggravated a problematic situation, but the third century in this respect is not when the problems started (Haas 2006: 276).

The economic situation that Cyprian describes, however, is corroborated by other types of sources. The number of inscriptions declined, as did building dedications. Fewer shipwrecks in the Mediterranean at the same time imply fewer ships, and less trade. The chronology of dated wood – which is very exact – shows that at least in western and southern Germany, building activity declined rapidly in the third century. In the same areas, archaeological finds in general followed the same pattern, with a peak in the early empire, and rapid decline in the third century. More exotic even is the often-cited lower metal contents in the Greenland icecap for the third century, when compared to the earlier Roman Empire, which indicates a decrease in the use of metal. Recently, even animal and human bones have been analysed, suggesting that in the third century people were smaller and therefore not as well nourished as in the previous period. Also, and more crucially, there was a substantial drop in the precious metal content of coins, which at first sight indicates unchecked inflation, with dire economic results (Jongman 2007: 187–95; Witschel 2004: 250).

Indeed, the monetary problems were such that in the West banks disappear from view altogether whereas in Egypt they continue to operate, notwithstanding a major crisis in AD 260, which is documented in a famous contemporary papyrus (**II 23** 1.411). The *strategos* Aurelius Ptolemaeus, a fairly high official, in charge of the administrative area (*nome*) of Oxyrhynchus, on 24 November AD 260 ordered exchange bankers to accept all genuine Roman imperial coinage, 'the divine coins of the empire', issuing a warning to businessmen to do the same. This means that they must have been unwilling to accept the coins without such an order. Prices in Egypt, on the other hand, were fairly stable up to AD 274, when papyri suddenly document a tenfold increase. This was followed by price stability, and is taken as evidence for devaluation by imperial decree, linked to the central currency reform known from Aurelian's reign. This reform meant that from now on the central denomination was not an increasingly debased silver coin, but a silver-clad coin. Looking at the monetary stability in Egypt for the remainder of the third century, it seems to have been a success. The necessity of changing the basis of a monetary system that went all the way back to Augustus betrays the level of debasement that had been going on in the earlier years of the third century. Indeed, whereas in the period between the reigns of Nero and Caracalla there was hardly more than 5 per cent deviation from the average weight of *aurei*, Rome's most valuable coins, in the third century, up to Aurelian's reform, there seemed hardly any standard left (Verboven 2007: 256). As the emperor had done when building the great wall surrounding Rome (**II 35**; see above, p. 16), Aurelian recognised that the Augustan system had come under too much stress and made innovations within it, rather than stretching it beyond its boundaries.

There may have been relative monetary stability in the later years of the third century, but in the northwest provinces, the number of coin hoards increased. This means that an increasing number of people buried their money in order to keep it safe in difficult circumstances, but then died before they were able to recover it (Howgego 1996: 88). This, along with other archaeological evidence, is used to indicate a demographic decline in the third century, worsened by the Antonine plague, and with agricultural land lying unused as a consequence (Jaillet 1996: 338). Fallow land was all the more problematic, since taxes had on the whole to be paid by towns on the basis of amounts of land. Wasteland was still taxed, increasing the pressure on the people cultivating the remaining land of an area. This could lead to land flight (*anachoresis*) by people unable to pay their taxes, as the people of Ağa Bey Köyü threatened to do in the above-mentioned petition (**II 17**). Stating that they would be unable to remain on the land and at the graves of their ancestors was not only a plea for mercy; it was also an implicit threat. If they were to leave the imperial estate, it too might become fallow land. The threat is even more explicit in the petition from the inhabitants of Skaptopara (**II 16 3.12336**). Towards the end of the third section of the text, the possibility that the inhabitants might flee their land is directly linked with the great loss in taxes that the Roman administration would suffer. These statements, it could be argued, need not only show despair in a dreadful situation; they might also be construed as the bargaining power that farmers had in times of demographic decline. Still, people could be either incited or forced to cultivate vacant plots, as had already been done by Hadrian in the early second and by Pertinax in the very late second century (Duncan-Jones 2004: 24). For a great many peasants in the third century, life was becoming increasingly harsh.

The Roman Empire, however, was vast and diverse. There were massive differences in the climates of Tunisia and southern Scotland, with very different agricultural systems as a result. Though in the third century many parts of the empire were in upheaval, not all areas were struck equally hard, nor did they all react in the same way, as the previous chapter has already indicated. In short, it is extremely difficult to make statements about the economic situation in the Roman Empire as a whole. Regional differentiation needs to be taken into account – as much of modern scholarship has argued. This applies even within relatively limited areas. For instance, survey archaeology in the Liris valley in Campania (**map 1**) shows that small rural sites disappear in the third century, indicating concentration of landholding by elites. Likewise, much further south, at San Giovanni di Ruoti, near Venosa (**map 1**), there were twenty-six rural sites for the period AD 70–220, of which only seven were still inhabited by the end of the third century. But evidence from another survey near Venosa (in an area with more fertile soil) shows that hardly any sites disappeared there in the third century. Still, there is a general trend in the third century on the Italian peninsula towards fewer sites (Duncan-Jones 2004: 28–31), although that does not necessarily indicate massive depopulation of the countryside. There were changes in the ownership of land – often meaning that peasants no longer lived on the land they cultivated – which meant that they escaped the attention of survey archaeologists. Some of the new villages that arose were quite well appointed, even owning baths (Witschel 2004: 263). Widening the scope dramatically, similar surveys of rural settlements in northern Syria, parts of Greece and Africa show a very different pattern. In the first two areas, there was rural increase, though

of course much land was laid waste in Syria as well, as the example of
Apamea (see above, p. 25) and further devastations by Shapur I (**II 10
5–9, 11–15**) make clear. In Africa, even more strikingly, the number of
sites increased almost continuously from the early second to the late
fifth century, whilst further evidence also suggests that in African cities
living standards remained generally high, with continuous building
activity (Duncan-Jones 2004: 34–5, figs 3–4; Mattingly and Hitchner
1995: 185). Economic life in Africa in the third century, it seems, was
more pleasant – or at least much less prone to change – than life on the
Italian peninsula, or in much of the rest of the empire.

Geographic differences become even more telling if they are
combined with chronological differentiation. Until the 260s, many
areas of the empire (especially those that were not directly touched
by warfare) changed little in terms of inhabitants, welfare and infra-
structure. The areas that have been thus defined by recent scholarship
include Italy, Gaul, Britain, Spain and of course northern Africa
(Witschel 1999, 2006: 145–9, 162–3). Likewise, as stated, papyri listing
prizes imply that until as late as 274 there was a reasonable stability of
prizes and that buying power of individuals may have increased –
notwithstanding the immense debasement and deviations in the
average weight of coins which became pronounced from the mid-third
century onwards (Verboven 2007: 256; de Blois 2002: 215–16; Rathbone
1996). Likewise, in Postumus' Gallic Empire the coins struck at the mint
of Trier remained of higher standard than the central coins struck by
Gallienus at the same time in the rest of the empire. This was especially
noticeable in the Gallic *aurei*, which not only had more gold in them,
but also were of superb stylistic quality. The same quality can be seen in
his other coins (**II 48 d**). These coins may even have been a sign of an
'image competition' between the two rulers (Drinkwater 1987: 155–7;
Hekster and Manders 2006). At one time or another, almost all areas of
the empire were struck by economic hardship. This, like brigandage
or the presence of soldiers, was not new in the third century. Indeed,
papyri from the Egyptian town of Thmouis tell the chilling story of a
village deserted by those who could no longer pay taxes, ransacked by
bandits, who were driven out by soldiers. The latter killed many of the
remaining villagers, after which plague made life even more miserable
(*P.Thmouis* I). In the third century, there were still areas that were
thriving, but they were fewer and fewer. Diocletian inherited an empire
in economic chaos (Rees 2004: 37–45), and the basis for this clearly lay
in the third century. But it needs to be remembered that not all areas
were equally chaotic. Often, as we saw at Skaptopara and Ağa Bey Köyü,

or indeed in earlier times in Thmouis, the armies were a factor in putting pressure on local economies. Increasingly, also, they became a factor in running the empire.

Armies, payments and economics

It may not be a coincidence that the area of the Roman world with the most stable economy was also the zone which suffered least from the military unrest in the empire. With the Mediterranean in the north, and the Sahara in the south, Africa was safe from enemy attacks. Brigands roamed round on occasion, but they had already done so before the third century, and created more embarrassment than disaster, as we saw in the previous chapter (**II 16 8.2728**). More importantly, perhaps, Africa was spared the large conglomeration of troops, which many border regions of the empire suffered (Witschel 2006: 146–53). For however devastating enemy troops could be, several scholars argue that an even greater scourge were the soldiers of the Roman armies themselves (Walbank 1969: 65). Certainly, in the third century soldiers were given privileges that had previously been thought to go against army discipline. Septimius Severus granted the soldiers the right to wear the gold rings that indicated equestrian rank, and to be married officially. More importantly even, he increased the soldiers' pay substantially. Herodian (**II 2 3.8.4–5**), with the advantage of hindsight, complains bitterly and directly links these measures to diminished military self-control and an increased longing for riches, though this may reflect a point to which Herodian paid particular attention (Zimmermann 1999). In any case, the ban on marriage had never restrained soldiers from starting families, but discarding the ban was an important ideological step, and it might not be coincidental that afterwards soldiers complained about serving far from their now official families (Potter 2004: 131).

Whatever the consequences may have been for military morale, the costs of the pay rise must have been staggering, leading to a shortage of precious metal with which to mint it. It has been argued that soldiers' pay had not really increased since the time of Domitian, and that the pay rise could be defended on that ground. The military, however, had in the meantime obtained the provision of free grain, and the increase in stipend was a real and dramatic extra cost, and may well have set a precedent. Soldiers were loyal to the man who paid them more than others (Potter 2004: 130). The comparison with Didius Julianus, who bought the emperorship from the praetorians, comes to mind (**II 1**

74.11.2; and see above, p. 13). Even Cassius Dio, who is not at all critical of Severus, having been one of the *amici* of the emperor (Millar 1964: 138–50), notes how desperately costs went out of control. In a passage (II 1 79.36) in which the emperor Macrinus is trying to keep the 'false Antoninus' (the later emperor Elagabalus; see above, p. 4) from the throne, he speaks explicitly about the Severans' undermining military discipline, and the impossibility of raising the money that the Severans' pay-rise had necessitated. Dio shifts the blame onto Caracalla (II 1 79.36.3), who is here referred to as Tarautus (the nickname of a particularly ugly, reckless, bloodthirsty and insignificant gladiator), and is referred to as a brother-killer for his murder of Geta (see below, pp. 48–9).

Whether Septimius Severus or his son were to blame is largely immaterial. At the beginning of the third century, soldiers obtained – and henceforth expected – more pay and privileges. In a period of economic turmoil, the consequences were difficult. Warfare itself, of course, also cost money, especially when matters became problematic. Shapur claimed, as we have seen above, that the treaty which Philip the Arab was forced to accept after the death of Gordian III meant that Philip paid off the Sassanids with 500,000 silver coins (*denarii*), and that in the ensuing battle against Decius the Romans lost 60,000 men (II 10 4; and see above, p. 19). This may have been an exaggeration. Numbers in sources from antiquity are notoriously unreliable. Also, the Romans certainly would not have agreed that they had become 'tributary' – though Sassanian superiority was emphasised in Sassanian state art (II 36). In any case, the figures mentioned show the financial strains the Roman Empire went through. This must explain the ongoing deterioration of the silver coinage up to Aurelian's currency reform, and the increase in number of imperial mints in a wide range of new locations. The latter development went hand in hand with the disappearance of local provincial coinage. Up to well into the third century, eastern cities expressed their economic and political autonomy, and indeed their identity, by minting their own coins. Sometime between the mid-century and Aurelian's reign, that stopped (Lo Cascio 2005: 161–2; cf. below, Chapter 3).

The problems with the armies were not just financial ones. Soldiers also became a common presence in areas where the military had previously been absent. Auxiliary units and legions were repeatedly transferred to deal with the difficulties at the frontiers. The many attempts at usurpation also caused soldiers to be moved throughout the realm. After all, generals who formed bonds with the soldiers could become a threat to the ruling emperor. The third century saw a great many examples of emperors being proclaimed by their troops (**II 4 27, 32; II 5 8.23, 9.1, 9.2, 9.6, 9.12**). Clearly, emperors had always been aware of the threat that the military could form. Dio Cassius (**II 1 80.4**), for instance, describes with horror how Elagabalus, here referred to as Avitus (**II 1 80.4.2**), rather than his customary 'false Antoninus', kills a number of men during his reign. The importance here lies not so much in the full list of names as in the 'official' reasons for their executions. Triccianus died for leading the Alban legion and Castinus for good generalship and being known to the soldiers (**II 1 80.4.3**); Sulla because he met up with soldiers from Gaul (**II 1 80.4.5**). In the case of Seius Carus, still according to Dio, associating with soldiers was a fabricated charge (**II 1 80.4.6**). If true, it would show more than anything how crucial the role of the soldiers was becoming. For linking oneself with soldiers must in that case have become a sufficient reason for execution. The many coins emphasising the loyalty of the troops (**II 45 a; II.48 c**, which claims *concordia militum*) indicate that such loyalty was no longer a given.

Much better, in such situations, to keep the soldiers on the move. This was necessary anyhow, if they were to fight in the many areas in which Rome was under threat. But soldiers travelling the Roman roads were bad news for those living in the vicinity, as has become clear from the petitions from Ağa Bey Köyü and Skaptopara (see above, p. 18). This had been the case before, as a papyrus from the reign of Hadrian shows (**II 19**). From that text it is evident that, even in Gibbon's happiest of times (see above, pp. 16–17), for many in the empire, life was not easy. Soldiers took what they wanted, with possible dire consequences for those whose belongings were confiscated. In the papyrus from Hadrian's reign, however, the prefect of Egypt clearly judges the abusing soldiers negatively, trying to block them from doing so again, and scolding them for harming the reputation of the military. From one papyrus, of course, it is impossible to say whether the actions of the prefect had any effect. Still, there is a marked difference from the reaction of Gordian III to the inhabitants of Skaptopara in the final section of that petition, where he simply sends them back to the governor (**II 16 3.12336**) (de Blois 2007: 506). New or not, to say that the behaviour of many soldiers was less than exemplary is an understatement. Soldiers confiscated and scavenged, and abused inhabitants of the areas they travelled through. As a result farmers fled their land (or at least threatened to do so). Others were killed by enemies (and Roman soldiers), or enlisted to make up for the shortfall of manpower which enemies and epidemics had caused (see above, p. 21). One long-term consequence was that food supply on campaign became problematic. Another consequence of these socio-economic upheavals was the coin deflation mentioned above (though other reasons, like increasing difficulties in mining gold and silver, also played a role). This in turn meant that the soldiers' pay lost its real value, leading to unrest amongst them.

Still, the armies were crucial to the safety of the empire. The empire survived the external threats on the eastern and northern borders as well as it did at least in part because battles were still won by the legions (approximately 165,000 men) and the increasing numbers of auxiliary troops (approximately 150,000 men). The latter consisted more than before of groups of people from the same ethnic background, occasionally 'barbaric' tribes, who retained their original mode of combat. In fact, detached units – with greater flexibility – became more important within the military structure, as did cavalry units (Campbell 2005b: 111–13). Most important, perhaps, was the fact that the emperor now fought with them. The accession of Maximinus Thrax, who was a soldier, made explicit how important the military role was for anyone who wanted to make a bid for the throne. This development, hardly surprisingly, had already started earlier. From Domitian onwards, emperors had led major campaigns in person, as had been done by generals or members of the imperial family under the Julio-Claudians and Vespasian. The emphasis on the emperor's military qualities is already clear from the great victory arch of Septimius Severus in the Forum Romanum, erected in AD 203, following Severus' triumph against the Parthians. Both the larger panels that adorn the arch and the underlying low-relief bands show the main events of the great city conquests of the years 194–5 and 197–9: siege, battle and the commander's address to the military (*adlocutio*) (**II 38a**). Throughout the imagery, soldiers and a group of officials are depicted as the core of the army as a fighting machine, with the emperor as general at its head. At the bases of freestanding columns, large sculptures show Roman soldiers holding chained Parthian prisoners (**II 38b**).

Similarly, the short military hairstyle with which most of the third-century emperors were portrayed emphasised their role as military men (**II 49d, e**; see below, Chapter 4) Emperors fought, at least in theory, alongside their men. And they had to be on campaign often, to deal with the multifaceted problems that threatened the empire. As a result, as we saw in Chapter 1, the position of Rome weakened. It also meant that emperors, more than before, surrounded themselves with equestrian men of military background. Even if Dio is simply blackening Caracalla when he describes how that emperor surrounded himself with soldiers, and gave them expensive gifts (**II 1** 78.9.1, 78.9.3), it would hardly be surprising if, in periods in which warfare was becoming more prominent, soldiers would gain easier access to the emperor. Rome had always worked with a system of personal patronage, in which a man's position depended at least in part on whom he knew. This was no third-century innovation, and it is once again worth stressing the continuity in the way the empire functioned. In practice, however, this traditional system now boosted the chances of gaining influence for military men over the chances for others to do so. Also, troops who were stationed in any particular area for a longer period of time would be a local force to be reckoned with. For different reasons, then, the importance of military men in administration was to increase in the third century.

Consequences of change

The petition from Skaptopara to Gordian III is often used, as it was above (p. 18), to show how badly soldiers behaved. Yet, noticeably, the inscription does not only show negative aspects of the military presence (**II 16** 3.12336). The man who brought the complaints to the emperor, as is clear from section II of the document, was a soldier who resided in the village. Similarly, around AD 245, during the reign of Philip the Arab, the villagers of Aragoe in Asia Minor sent a soldier, a certain Didymus, to present the emperor with a petition, after abuse by soldiers and military officers (*CIL* 3.14191; Hauken 1998: 150–3). A century earlier, such protests were most likely to have been brought forward by an orator. Now military men had taken on that function. This may partly be the result of the growing links between soldiers and the territory in which they were based. As stated above, soldiers could now officially establish families, and thus more than before become part of a local community – for which they would be willing to undertake action. People work together with those whom they see on a daily basis. Furthermore, the position of traditional local elites in areas with a strong military presence may have become somewhat eroded. These, as stated above, were zones in which land was trampled, products were taken to feed the army, and land ended up lying fallow. This made it more difficult for those whose finances depended on the land to continue their traditional modes of financial patronage. Increasingly, even members of the elite had to dodge their financial obligations (see below, Chapter 3). Finally, in a period in which soldiers had become the most obvious protectors of the empire, it made sense to turn to the military for help.

At a higher level, as is described above as well, this 'who you see is who you help' notion also functioned. Emperors increasingly surrounded themselves with military men. Again, however, this growing influence of soldiers on the emperor in a period of war was nothing new. When Marcus Aurelius was engaged in extensive warfare in the second half of the second century, he appointed career soldiers to posts of importance. One of them, T. Varius Clemens, was even made the official responsible for the imperial correspondence (*ab epistulis*), and in that capacity apparently in a supreme position to advise the emperor whom to appoint to important positions. Unsurprisingly, he guaranteed other equestrian military men social and political progress (Birley 1992). In the third century, through actual warfare, military logistics, drastic requisitioning of food, goods and services, and the restoration of law and order in war-ridden areas, many emperors spent much of their time in war zones, forging bonds with military men and imperial staff acting in the provinces. The imperial government needed new types of skills, mainly provided by the military middle cadre, who in this way obtained access to higher functions (de Blois 2001b).

Eventually, senators would even be excluded from governing provinces with military problems, and professional soldiers would command the armies. The two are of course related, and must be seen as an attempt to make sure that in these times of military insecurity the armies had generals with a long and thorough military background. It was promoting equestrians over senators not so much because of their rank as because of their skills (Lo Cascio 2005: 159). Famously, Aurelius Victor blames the emperor Gallienus for issuing an edict forbidding senators to take military appointments (**II 4 33, 37**). There is, in fact some evidence that from Gallienus' reign onwards certain military posts disappeared from senatorial career inscriptions and that military commands were increasingly given to non-senators. This was, however, similar to Marcus' policies as set out above, and notwithstanding Victor's statement, there seems not to have been an actual edict by the emperor, even if he did promote equestrians to provinces where the governor had previously been a senator, and no longer appointed senators as legates of the legions (Christol 1986: 38–48; de Blois 1976: 57–83). Victor's statement, in any case, betrays a lack of awareness of imperial reality. Equestrians could threaten Gallienus' position as well as senators – as the reign of Maximinus Thrax must have made clear.

Still, Aurelius Victor's notion of an edict by Gallienus is understandable in the context of that emperor's actions. More than almost anyone before him, Gallienus changed some of the military and administrative structures of the empire. First, he created a special cavalry unit, which was independent of the legions and directly linked to the emperor in person. This *comitatus*, which was based at Milan, could be moved around much more easily. Milan itself was, secondly, fortified, as were some other strategically important localities such as Aquileia, also in northern Italy (**map 1**). These fortified areas were, thirdly, defended by new garrisons of soldiers who were detached from different legions. Gallienus, in this way, raised military forces outside of the normal command structure. This, together with his tendency to appoint capable equestrians as commanders of legions, or as a *dux* commanding the new garrison, created a much more flexible system of defence, foreshadowing the defence system of the later empire (Campbell 2005b: 115; Potter 2004: 257–8; de Blois 1976: 30–4). It must also have annoyed senators, who were *de facto* if not *de jure* excluded from many important offices.

Aurelius Victor was not entirely wrong. Yet he was not entirely right either. In provinces like Africa, where there were no long-term problems, loyal senators kept fulfilling governorships. Equally, non-militarily important positions in Rome and Italy went to members of the traditional elite. This may have eased their annoyance somewhat (Mennen 2007). Still, they were in most respects surpassed by new men for major offices.

These new men, and indeed the new bodies of troops, were directly loyal to the emperor. And ever more often, equestrian commanders with special commands were sent to the provinces in which fighting had to take place. When problems were substantial (which was often, as Chapter 1 shows) there was even a tendency to unify military action beyond the province boundaries. These occasional 'provinces of war' were under the command of single individuals (Lo Cascio 2005: 161). Such individuals were men the emperor could trust – often direct family – or 'local heroes' who had in practice gained the upper hand in an area under threat, such as the 'restorer of the whole East', Odaenathus (II 14 2.3946; see above, pp. 23–4). In the case of Odaenathus, the centre clearly lost control, but in general these new types of appointment strengthened central imperial control. These new appointment structures, in the course of the century and beyond it, would lead to a new organisation of official titulature. This new organisation, like so much of what happened in the third century, had already started under Marcus Aurelius. It now became more pronounced. Those with close links to the imperial court were addressed as *perfectissimus*, and this status became the important one to have (Potter 2004: 258). There is even some indication that certain equestrian posts carried as much weight as senatorial offices, if not more. One could interpret in this way the career inscriptions of Marcus Cnaeus Licinius Rufinus, which place his equestrian status before his senatorial rank (Millar 1999: 94–5).

Similar growth of central influence happened in tranquil areas like Africa, notwithstanding the continuous appointment of senators there, through the expansion of imperial estates. The emperors had always owned land all over the empire. Over time, through inheritance or direct acquisition, these had grown immense and were an important source of wealth for the emperor. This property was run by (equestrian) procurators, who were direct appointments of the *princeps* and for that reason could have disproportionate influence on the running of the province in which these estates were placed. Ağa Bey Köyü, for instance, was such an estate (**II 17**), and it was the procurator whom they first approached with their problems. This makes their threat, in the last lines, to abandon the estate (see above, p. 34) all the more problematic for the emperor – he was to lose direct income if the land on his estate became fallow. Through both military and non-military appointments, then, the centre became more important in running the periphery (Garnsey 2004: 148), though curiously enough at the same time the importance of the city of Rome diminished (see above, Chapter 1). This new, more 'central' government in times of military upheaval, with its systematizing of offices, seems to have led to diminished leniency from those who held office.

Ramsay MacMullen, who has written insightful work on almost all periods of imperial history, pointed out about twenty years ago how this came about, though he was discussing a period successive to the one central here:

> But when appointive rank hardened into its own structure of honors, rewards and promotions that increasingly controlled a man's decisions, constituting his whole life, and when the imperial authority he represented became gradually inflated and godlike, then he could feel no sympathy for disobedient subjects. They were compelled to behave. Whatever force was needed should be used. So I imagine the process of change. (MacMullen 1988: 139)

The third century did not yet have the rigid structure of promotions that would characterise the later empire, and the 'inflated' authority of the emperor was only gradually becoming 'godlike' (see below,

Chapter 4). But the process which MacMullen described took shape in the third century. In AD 278, for the first time in Roman history, disobedience to the edict of a ranking official was deemed a capital crime. Not adhering to a decision about labour on dikes was grounds for execution (MacMullen 1988: 139). For this, there is no precedent, and it shows that notwithstanding all visible continuity, there was real transformation as well. The number of military men that people living in towns would encounter grew, especially in towns that were near battlegrounds (MacMullen 1988: 145) but also increasingly in Rome and the Italian peninsula (Busch 2007: 315–16, 341). Different people now had to be approached when one was in trouble, and their reactions could not always be anticipated. Of course, these changes appear minor as compared to those encountered by people who, as we have seen (Chapter 1), were deported or lost all of their possessions when whole cities were destroyed in the many wars that were fought. And not all administrative changes were disadvantageous to the inhabitants of the empire. Notwithstanding all the misery, the third century also saw a development that would strengthen the unity of the empire, and would have profound effects on the Roman world. Indeed, the consequences of the development of Roman law would long outlast even the fall of the Roman Empire.

CHAPTER 3

Law and Citizenship

In the third century there may have been economic problems in the empire, and administrative changes which led to severe difficulties at local levels, but it was not all gloom. In fact, AD 212 saw one of the most important steps in the unification of the empire. In that year, the emperor Caracalla declared (nearly) all free inhabitants of the Roman Empire to be Roman citizens in the so-called *Constitutio Antoniniana*. This was a move with major consequences, not the least of which was a change to the status of Roman law. Yet this important change is only marginally mentioned in the literary sources. Single phrases by the lawyer Ulpian (in the *Digest* assembled much later, which lists the names of the original author of a statement) and by Dio Cassius, together with some later references, make clear that it was Caracalla who decreed this (**II 21 1.5.17; II 1 78.9.5**). Discussion is, however, still fierce over the details of the measure.

In this discussion, much emphasis has been on part of a heavily restored papyrus text, which was reported in 1902 and published in 1910 (**II 20**). From its publication onwards, scholars have argued over almost every part of the papyrus, including the question of whether or not the text is a Greek translation of the *Constitutio*. In 1962, a list was created of some ninety major discussions on Caracalla's edict, most of which are still current (Sasse 1962). There is, however, current consensus on the fact that what we have in the papyrus is part of the original text. That makes it an important document, though not all agree on this:

> The document has added little to the understanding of this act of Caracalla, which can be evaluated independently of the papyrus … This remarkable controversy, which has added singularly little to historical knowledge, has been concerned more with the formulation of Caracalla's pronouncement, his motives and intentions, than with the practical effects of it in the Roman world. (Sherwin-White 1973[2]: 279, 380)

These words, by one of the great twentieth-century scholars working on Roman administration, show the two different directions of scholarship which are possible when analysing the *Constitutio Antoniniana*: one choice is to look at 'the practical effects of it in the Roman world' whilst another is to examine the emperor's 'motives and intentions'. Notwithstanding Sherwin-White's damming criticism in this instance, the latter exercise is useful in its own right, and for this the papyrus is of the utmost importance. In fact, both the effects of Caracalla's remarkable measure and its intentions are amongst the most debated aspects of third-century history. As with all historical events, however, the issuing of the *Constitutio Antoniniana* should be seen in the context of its time.

Lawyers and politics

The Severan dynasty, up to the death of Severus Alexander in AD 235, is commonly seen as the great age of jurists. Famous jurists like Papinianus, Paul, Messius, Ulpian and Modestinus not only became classic authors, but also reached important administrative positions; some of them even became praetorian prefect, which office, even after the military and administrative changes that were discussed in the previous chapter, remained the highest position for non-senators in the Roman Empire (Syme 1970; de Blois 2001b: 138–40). This age of jurists did not, however, last long. Aemilius Papinianus, who became praetorian prefect in AD 205, was the first jurist to gain such high office and Herennius Modestinus, who died sometime after AD 239, can be considered to be the last. As we saw above, from the second half of the third century onwards, other people – with more military and logistical experience – gained influence in the imperial administration.

It was during the high tide of Roman jurists that the *Constitutio Antoniniana* was proclaimed, which one should keep in mind. The rise and fall of Roman jurists, however, is also telling in its own right. The factors underlying their rise can be roughly summarised as follows (de Blois 2001b: 144–58). First, and most simply, by the third century there were so many legal appeals made to the centre that specialists were needed to deal with them. Specifically, it became common to appoint one praetorian prefect with legal knowledge, and one with military experience (Honoré 1982: 3). Secondly, the emperor Septimius Severus himself seems to have been particularly interested in law (Zwalve 2001: 159–62). Imperial interest tended to have empire-wide consequences, and the boost to the jurists' standing might well follow from the emperor's patronage. That patronage may have had a knock-on effect.

If the emperor supported jurists, others would do so too. In this way, jurists became part of the emperor's urban entourage – a reciprocal network in which positions were bestowed through mutual recommendations. As we saw above, the absence from Rome of later third-century emperors combined with the changing needs for running the empire explains the problems for later third-century jurists. Soldiers became central in the emperors' more peripheral entourage. It was again not the system of patronage which changed, but the people who stood in the best position to profit from it. The imperial absence from Rome also meant that many judicial tasks of the emperors, which had first been dealt with by high-placed jurists, were now taken over by 'deputy-emperors' (*iudices vice sacra*). These men used jurists for advice, but took the need for jurists in high positions away (Peachin 1996: 164; de Blois 2001b: 148). As we have seen before, what at first sight looked like a massive rupture was in fact only a combination of smaller transitions. Jurists did not disappear, but became less visible in more subordinate functions. The system of patronage, which had temporarily boosted their fortunes, now boosted other fortunes. There is no denying that there was change, but there was continuity within the system as well.

Purpose of the *Constitutio Antoniniana*

The *Constitutio Antoniniana* made all free inhabitants of the empire Roman citizens with the exception of the so-called *dediticii*. These were people who became subject to Rome through a formal surrender in war, and certain freed slaves (though there is discussion on the exact definition, as on almost everything linked to the edict). Since Roman citizens were bound by Roman law, a consequence was that one legal system applied to almost all inhabitants of one of the larger empires in world history: 'From a municipal system that took account of the law common to various Mediterranean peoples, the *ius gentium*, it became the *ius civile*. Roman law now purported to apply to the whole civilized world, claiming to be founded on reason and a basic nature shared by all' (Honoré 2004: 113). This fits well with a high tide for legal specialists, and Ulpian at least seems to have promoted the edict. Yet it is extremely unlikely that this was its primary purpose. There are, in fact, two possible reasons for the *Constitutio Antoniniana* which are explicitly stated in the ancient sources. Dio Cassius (**II 1 78.9.4–5**), as always extremely critical of Caracalla, whom he blames for having pampered the soldiers (see above, p. 37), mentions the most mundane of them, arguing that the whole exercise was really a hidden tax-raising measure. Though it is true that Caracalla's financial situation was problematic, not least because the emperor (or his father) had substantially raised the soldiers' pay (see above, p. 36), this is not a sufficient argument. Few of those who had not gained citizenship in the previous centuries would have been wealthy, whilst the inheritance tax, which is most often stressed as an important new revenue, had already existed at least in Egypt, and possibly in other provinces as well (Sherwin-White 1973[2]: 281). Dio's comment is also suspect since it fits all too well in a long literary tradition – especially strong in the third century – of complaining about the burdens of taxation, and of imperial abuse of the money that was raised through these taxations. Finally, even if Dio's statement is correct, it seems not to have told the full story.

The second motive may have been mentioned by Caracalla himself, on the papyrus with the Greek translation of the text. He states that the edict is an appeasement to the gods, who had saved him from a conspiracy. It needs to be emphasised, though, that the actual words 'when that conspiracy occurred' are reconstructed by the editor of the papyrus. The conspiracy in question, in any case, should perhaps better be defined as a coup. Septimius Severus had left the empire in the hands of his sons Caracalla and Geta, but the two famously did not get along, both vying for sole power. Septimius' renowned last words, as described by Dio (II 1 77.15.2), had a certain irony in them, since the brothers turned out to be all but 'harmonious'. Herodian (II 2 4.4), who was a contemporary, describes the situation at length, though he may well have embellished a number of aspects of the story for rhetorical effect. He suggests a situation in which the two emperors blocked each other at every possible turn, and even if only a fraction of that description is true, life at the court must have been very difficult indeed. In December 211, Caracalla eventually killed his brother. A melodramatic scene in Herodian's text states how Geta was stabbed whilst their mother, Julia Domna, held him. Caracalla lost no time, but instantly sought the support of the praetorians – being aware that the support of these soldiers was crucial if he was to remain in power. Interestingly, Herodian then states how Caracalla went into the sanctuary of the praetorians, and started to make 'sacrifices in gratitude for his deliverance'. This, of course, is exactly what the Greek papyrus states as the reason for bestowing citizenship on the inhabitants of the empire. In the aftermath, Caracalla killed a large number of Geta's supporters (including the jurist Papinianus), and promised, as Herodian states, very substantial amounts of money to his own supporters. This must have further worsened the financial problems he was in.

Caracalla also had Geta's memory condemned. This *damnatio memoriae* was carried out throughout the empire – Geta's name was chiselled out from an enormous number of texts such as milestones and more massive monuments. Famously, for instance, the image and name of Geta were removed from the so-called Arco degli Argentarii in Rome, after which the surface of the monument was smoothed over so as to leave as little trace as possible (**II 39 a, b**). The *damnatio* even applied to papyri (**II 22**). A birth certificate for the son of a certain Marcus Lucretius Diogenes, named Herennas, which can be dated to AD 209, mentions Septimius Severus (who was emperor at the time) and his two sons. But Geta's name was later deleted from the document (made visible in II 22 by the name's being struck through; de Jong 2007: 103–4). The erasure of Geta's memory was probably as fierce as it was because fratricide could only be condoned if the murdered brother had been a monster, who had conspired against him. Granting citizenship to all his subjects so that they could share in his good fortune and offer to the gods on his behalf, so Caracalla argued, was his way of thanking the gods for preserving him from this 'conspiracy'. For such an important victory only the great gods could be responsible, and they had to be repaid through similar greatness. Only the full 'majesty of the Roman people' would do.

To these explicitly mentioned motives, others can and have been added. Granting citizenship to all may have been a way to boost Roman identity. All subjects of Rome were to become truly 'Romans' – setting them far above the invaders who were to disturb Roman borders. It also gave clear political advantages to Caracalla, not only by explaining Geta's *damnatio memoriae*, but also by making a dramatic statement at the beginning of his reign that cost little money (and perhaps gained him substantial sums), and creating bonds with many subjects, who were to become his namesakes, since Roman tradition dictated that new citizens were named after the man who promoted their citizenship (Potter 2004: 139). All of these motives, however, as stated in a recent article by one of the foremost scholars of Roman law, point 'at best to the occasion of, not the deeper causes of, the extension of citizenship. It is like explaining the grant to Scotland of a separate Parliament with its own powers of legislation as a tactical move by the Labour party to secure Scottish seats in the general election of 1997' (Honoré 2004: 114).

Whatever the direct purpose of the *Constitutio Antoniniana*, its causes ran deeper. The periphery was becoming central to the empire, with jurists, senators and even emperors coming increasingly from, and spending much of their time, outside of Rome (see above, Chapter 1). The role of traditional senatorial families was diminishing (even if their status continued), and through the edict, millions could now hold public office who could not have done so before AD 212. Finally, citizenship had already expanded substantially over the centuries. Giving citizenship to all could be seen as a logical (though still radical) next step. Unless more straightforward sources of information are found, the 'true' purpose of the edict will remain shrouded in mystery. For now, it needs to be emphasised that the different purposes mentioned above are not mutually exclusive. A combination of them seems the most likely explanation for Caracalla's actions in AD 212.

Consequences of the *Constitutio Antoniniana*

As mentioned above, 'motives and intentions' are one part of the debate surrounding the *Constitutio*. Its practical effects are another. The most obvious of these effects was, as stated, the fact that almost all free inhabitants of the empire became citizens overnight. Roman citizens had three names (the *tria nomina*), their *praenomen* (first name), *nomen gentile* (name of the *gens*) and *cognomen* (nickname). It was customary for someone becoming citizen to use as their *nomen gentile* the name of the person who bestowed this new status on them. Many of the new citizens of AD 212 therefore adopted the emperor's name (Aurelius) as their gentile name. Aurelius became the most common name in the East of the empire, and ran a close second to the name Julius (which had been established for centuries) in the West. In the register of the praetorians in Rome of July 210 (*CIL* 6.1058) there were only thirty-nine Aurelii out of 802 names (c. 5 per cent), whereas nineteen out of twenty names from the same register on June 227 are Aurelius (*CIL* 6.2799). One papyrus from an auxiliary fort in Dura Europos, truly the empire's furthest corner, shows how from AD 193 to 212 there were eight Aurelii, twelve other Romans, and thirty-three non-Roman names, whereas from AD 214 to 217 it lists fifty-five Aurelii versus nineteen other names (*P.Dura* 98). There were even people who had already held Roman citizenship before the edict and still added Aurelius to their names, although there were also inhabitants (especially many peasants) who continued to use their old name (**II 23 10.1274**; and see below, p. 53). Apparently there was some lack of clarity on how to implement the *Constitutio*, giving rise to local variation (Sherwin-White 1973[2]: 386–7; Salway 1994: 133–6).

The changes in names also seem to indicate a growing sense of being Roman – at least for the new citizens. Specific tokens of Roman-ness can for instance be found in as remote a place as Palmyra, where shortly after the *Constitutio Antoniniana* a (perhaps new) Roman citizen explicitly had himself depicted in a toga – the ultimate symbol of Roman status – on his sarcophagus (**II 40**) (Schmidt-Colinet and al-As'ad, in press). He is the central figure making the offering. Similarly, a life-size portrait from Commagene, from the area near Nemrud Dağ, shows a young man with short beard and moustache (**II 41**). The style is somewhat provincial, but the scene it depicts is Roman. For in the portrait, the man is clearly visible with his head covered (*capite velato*). Covering the head with a toga whilst performing ritual is a very Roman tradition. The portrait has been dated to Caracalla's reign, which would form an indication that after obtaining Roman citizenship this Syrian young man started even to worship the gods in Syria by Roman methods (Simon 1995). Even a whole city could respond to the new situation. In the Egyptian town Ptolemais Euergetis in the Fayum area, for instance, a temple to Zeus Kapitolios was rapidly constructed, clearly referring to the supreme god of Rome who was worshipped on the Capitol. This cult had previously been common only in towns with a special link to Rome, and is the only example of a cult to a clearly Roman god in Egypt – using a mainly Roman ritual calendar. In this temple to the new Roman-nesss, however, local traditions were not forgotten. There were festivals to the crocodile god Souchos, to Harpokrates, Sarapis and the Nile; all specifically Egyptian gods (Beard et al. 1998: 362–3). This local religious response to the *Constitutio Antoniniana* is characterised by the same mixture of rupture and continuity which seems to define third-century developments. Local identity was reshaped by everyone legally becoming Roman, but it did not disappear.

Possibly the most eloquent testimony to this is a local coin minted at Tyre (Phoenicia) during the reign of Gordian III (**II 44**). Its obverse shows the emperor, with standard Latin titulature, but on its reverse the coin depicts the local myth of Dido founding Carthage, with the Greek name 'Dido' in the Greek alphabet, and her Phoenician name 'Elishar' in Phoenician. Being Roman went hand in hand with remaining Greek and Phoenician (Howgego 2005: 14). Local coinage is, in fact, an ideal source type for analysing the relationship between Roman and local identities. Yet, as could perhaps have been expected from the ongoing 'centralisation' of offices, the third century saw a slow but sure disappearance of provincial cities minting their own coins. The political and military instability and the proliferation of imperial mints at different places will have played a role in this (see above, Chapter 2), but central attempts to present the realm as unified and whole will also have been of importance. How otherwise to explain that henceforward 'the Genius of the Roman people *in Latin* [was] chosen as the symbol for the whole empire' (Howgego 2005: 16)?

When looking at the consequences of the *Constitutio Antoniniana* for the development of Roman law, again a mixture between Roman and local habits can be observed. Numerous local customs continued, without the Roman administration trying to impose Roman law from one day to the next. The importance of tradition for the Romans applied to law as well, and both before and after the universalisation of Roman law, jurists stressed the importance of local customs explicitly (**II 21** 1.3.33, 1.3.40). Custom supplemented Roman law, as stated by the high-profile jurists Ulpian and Modestinus, who both emphasise the importance of custom as a source of law. No emperor – not even Caracalla – issued an edict that Roman law should be applied everywhere.

In the period directly following the issuing of the *Constitutio*, groups who might have been disadvantaged by the new legal reality could have their ancient rights confirmed. That at least, unsurprisingly, happened to the military. Soldiers had always had specific (much more lenient) rules for validating their wills, and – in some cases – the new situation could put an end to that. Immediately, a case about the inheritance of a soldier, the brother of a certain Florus, was put forward to the imperial chancery to test the ground. Caracalla decided that in this case common law did not apply. For soldiers, all remained as it had always been (Zwalve 2007: 367–72). Furthermore, the *Constitutio Antoniniana* seems to have had an explicit clause guaranteeing the rights of local laws. Also, there were few experts in Roman law in the Greek East, hindering the Romanisation of local law (Garnsey 2004: 146–7). For instance, Gregory Thaumaturgus (c. 213–75), who was converted to Christianity by the great philosopher Origen, and became an important example for later Christians, studied law in Beirut. Even he found it burdensome that Roman law was all in Latin. But he also commented that all who wanted to have a career in the imperial administration now tried to get into the Beirut law school. Roman law was there for the long run, and the old rhetorical institutions of Antioch, Athens and Alexandria saw their position weakened (Zwalve 2007: 371). For quite some time after the *Constitutio* was issued, there seems to have been a transitional period in which Roman law and provincial rules remained mixed. There were no concerted efforts to bring Roman law to all levels of provincial society (Cotton 1993). Still, Roman private law seeped through into daily practice, even if it was understood differently from one place to another (Stolte 2001: 176–7). There may be much discussion about *how* general citizenship boosted Roman law, but it seems clear that it did.

In Egypt, for instance, after AD 212 women could apply to the prefect to be granted their right to act without a guardian. It was much easier for Roman citizen women to gain this *ius liberorum*, which carried with it also inheritance rights. In order to obtain this status, a citizen woman needed to have three children, and would probably have needed to prove the existence of her children. Illuminating is the papyrus (**II 23 12.1467**) of the Egyptian Aurelia Thaisous, who also uses the Greek name Lolliane. Greek was a common language in Egypt, and having names in two languages was not exceptional. Nor, in the light of the *Constitutio Antoniniana*, is the name Aurelia surprising. This Lolliane wrote to the prefect in AD 263, applying for her right to transact business on her own and asking the prefect's office to make sure there would be no problems. She emphasised that she was able to write herself. This was no necessity for acting without a guardian, but it did show her independence. The office filed her application – presumably to be able to refer to it if any questions arose. As it happens, a later papyrus records how Aurelia Thaisous conducted business and explicitly referred to her *ius liberorum* (*P.Oxy.* 12.475; Pestman 1994: 245).

Even if women did not have three children and could not apply for their legal independence, Roman law was present. A papyrus from the mid-third century (**II 23 10.1274**) describes the situation of a certain Aurelia Aristous who lost her husband Achillion and had a guardian appointed 'according to Roman custom'. Striking is the dominance of 'Aurelius' in the names of all concerned, and again the use of double names, one of which is in Greek. The late husband, however, seems not to have used his Roman name, although he fulfilled a not unimportant function, as *basilicogrammateus* (the deputy of the *strategos*) in the area near Alexandria. The papyrus, like the one discussed above, also shows the high-level administrative organisation of Egypt, carefully registering property and information on the rights of individuals. The Laetorian law which is spoken of was an old Roman law to protect under-age individuals against financial abuse. It made void any debts contracted under the age of twenty-five.

The high-level organisation, and indeed Roman citizenship, could also be problematic. After Caracalla's great reform, more people than before were obliged to take up public office. This of course raised one's status, but was also highly expensive. One sign of the financial difficulties for many in the third century was an increasing tendency to dodge these expensive obligations. Members of local elites were no longer willing or able to continue the tasks they had undertaken in the early empire. One way in which this wide-ranging phenomenon becomes visible is, again, in Egyptian papyri. From the *Constitutio Antoniniana* onwards, property was increasingly bought in women's names. When men had a certain amount of property, after all, they would have to take up public obligations. Forfeiting these obligations would result in confiscation of that very property. Women, however, could not hold office, and placing property in female hands was a mode of escaping unwelcome duties, though the legality of the construction could be questioned. An AD 223 papyrus, written on behalf of a woman named Julia Dionysia from Oxyrhynchus, makes clear that the construction was suspect (**II 23 1.77**). The highest-ranking local official (*gymnasiarch*) of the town, Aurelius Ammonius, was as *prytanis* responsible for appointing men to take up public office. He apparently questioned whether Julia's husband did not in fact own more property than was officially stated, which would have meant that he could be nominated for a suitable office. Julia Dionysia had already sent petitions to Ammonius declaring that a specific house was hers and not her husband's, but clearly she had to reiterate that claim, under oath, to satisfy the *gymnasiarch* that nothing had been falsified (Bassiouni 1989: 239–41). Whether or not Julia spoke the truth is immaterial in the greater scheme of things. The number of papyri emphasising that certain possessions really did not belong to the man of the household indicates that substantial numbers of people were trying to use a loophole to get out of new obligations.

At the same time, this must have strengthened the position of women, who now obtained more property in their own right. Roman citizenship thus sometimes bolstered women's rights. On the other hand, Roman law sometimes made women's position worse than it had been under local law. For instance, Severus and Caracalla issued a law in AD 197 which stated that women could not accuse men of adultery (*CJ* 9.9.1), which under local law they sometimes could. Still, more far-reaching laws on adultery were cancelled because there were too many indictments (**II 1 77.16.4**), as Dio experienced first-hand when he was consul. Caracalla's personal behaviour cannot have promoted conformity with the laws (**II 1 78.16.4**), though perhaps Dio's story to this effect should not be taken at face value, since he accuses all emperors that he dislikes of sexual abuse.

Two more indirect consequences of the *Constitutio Antoniniana* should be mentioned, both of them important for the functioning of the empire post-AD 212. One is related to religion (and indeed the worship of the emperor) and will resurface more extensively in the next two chapters. In short, the enlargement of Roman citizenship made the Roman gods and the Roman emperor more central than they were before and to an extent paved the way for edicts like the one of Trajan Decius in AD 249, which ordered all inhabitants of the empire to sacrifice to Roman gods and started the first empire-wide persecution of Christians. A second consequence is related to the increased sense of being Roman, already mentioned above. It was this increased Roman-ness which made inhabitants more part of the empire than ever before. Though this never did fully replace local identity, it made rebellion against the empire from within less likely. It is perhaps more than coincidental that, as mentioned above (Chapter 1), the only two surviving inscriptions which are 'for the safety of the empire' stem from the third century, and are from the periphery. One is from Apulum, in modern Romania (*AE* 1965.30), whilst the other is from the area near Cologne (**II 16 13.7844**). As stated, the inscriptions are important because they show that at least some people felt the empire to be under sufficient threat to sacrifice on its behalf. But equally, they show that the empire as such had become a clear entity, in which all inhabitants took part. Even Postumus' Gallic Empire (see above, Chapter 1) was organised as if it were still Roman. The *Constitutio Antoniniana* as such is mentioned only in very few literary sources. But its direct and indirect consequences are many and become evident through different types of sources. If nothing else, this should be a warning that the absence of literary evidence about an event does not necessarily mean that the event was unimportant. Absence of evidence, as is well known, is no evidence of absence.

CHAPTER 4

Development and Perception of Emperorship

To a large extent, Roman imperial history was defined by emperors – at least in the eyes of the Romans themselves. This can be said to have started as early as Augustus' reign, with the emphasis in contemporary writing on the first *princeps*, and was made abundantly clear by the time of the second century. Suetonius wrote biography, and therefore divided history into the different members of the ruling dynasty, whilst Tacitus – apologetically – pointed out how 'with equality cast aside, all looked to the orders of the princeps' (Tacitus *Annales* 1.4). It is, therefore, not surprising not only that the changes described in the previous chapters had a profound effect on the development of emperorship, but that this aspect of third-century history has received abundant attention. In brief, two points stand out when looking at emperors from AD 193 to AD 284. Firstly, there were very many of them. Secondly, most of them were soldiers. These obvious observations, however, hide further (and perhaps more far-reaching) developments.

At the end of the period under discussion, there had been a major shift away from emperorship as it was defined in the first and second centuries. Under the Tetrarchs, individual imperial features were suppressed in imagery, to emphasise the cohesion of the imperial college, with much attention given to divine aspects of rule (Rees 2004: 46–56). Two emperors (*Augusti*) and their second-in-commands (*Caesares*) were presented as a homogeneous group of (near-)divine rulers. If one compares this with earlier, highly individualised presentations in which – on the whole – imperial divinity is mentioned much more subtly, if at all, the change becomes apparent. Again, as with the development of citizenship and the position of Rome, there appears at first sight to have been a massive rupture from the beginning of the period under discussion to its end. Yet, as before, change took place gradually, with much emphasis on continuity. It is hardly surprising that imperial representation changed in a period which was characterised by a lack of stable and clearly established central power; in which various rulers, with different degrees of success, tried to establish control over the empire, and deal with its crises. In the third century, it became increasingly difficult to present the emperor as the natural focal point of society, since his position was hardly ever unchallenged. Yet the emperor's role as focal point was instrumental in keeping the empire together (Hopkins 1978: 197–242; Ando 2000: 373–405), and emperors often emphasised their traditionalism – even, or especially, in the face of overwhelming evidence to the contrary. How, then, did the change come about?

Soldier emperors?

Describing the events of AD 69, the year of the four emperors, Tacitus famously stated that 'the secret of the empire was now disclosed, that an emperor could be made elsewhere than at Rome' (Tacitus *Histories* 1.4). This became abundantly clear in the third century, culminating in Carus' decision not even to ask for acclamation in the Roman senate. The regular attempts by army units to make their commander the supreme commander of the realm – outside of Rome – are indeed often seen as the key characteristic of emperorship in the period from Severus Alexander to Diocletian. As was stated in an influential thesis on the so-called 'awful revolution': 'the theory of an elected emperor was a constant incitement to ambitious army leaders, and these were frequently able to exploit the devotion of the troops to whom the State as an object of allegiance was meaningless' (Walbank 1969: 64). Michael Rostovtzeff, in one of the seminal works of twentieth-century scholarship on the ancient world, went even further and spoke of:

> a systematic militarization of government ... A militarized bureaucracy was the watchword, and at the head of this bureaucracy a monarch with autocratic power, hereditary in his family, his power being based on the allegiance of the army and the state officials and on the personal worship of the emperor ... [the old upper classes] were replaced by a new military aristocracy. Like the emperors themselves, this aristocracy sprang from the ranks of the Roman army and, like the emperors, it was subject to perpetual change. (Rostovtzeff 1957²: 448–9)

The idea of soldier emperors, acclaimed by their troops, fighting against each other and external enemies, dying (stabbed in the back) on the battlefield, remains a popular one, as testified by the title *Soldatenkaiser* (soldier emperors) for a recent short history of the third century (Sommer 2004).

Of course there is truth in the notion. But becoming emperor through military acclamation was nothing new. Amongst emperors who gained power in this way are well-established 'good' emperors such as Vespasian and Septimius Severus. Even Nerva's adoption of Trajan in AD 97 may well have resulted from military pressures (Bennett 2001[2]: 46–7). Famously, emperors tended to start their letters to the senate with the words: 'I and the legions are in good health', and a well-known anecdote recounts how, when the rhetorician Favorinus was reproached by friends for yielding to Hadrian in a matter of grammar though being in the right, he responded that the 'most learned man is the one who has thirty legions' (Hekster 2007: 91). The real change in the third century, at least from the death of Severus Alexander onwards, was that – through the sheer number of usurpers – ruling emperors no longer managed to impose themselves and their dynasty for any considerable length of time. Military qualities appeared to have become *sufficient* qualities to gain the purple, rather than just *necessary* ones. Yet that the emperors as a group could with some justification be described as 'soldier emperors' does not mean that individual emperors wanted to be so described, nor that views on what an emperor ought to be changed alongside common practice.

In order to find out how, in fact, emperors wanted to be seen, central Roman coinage is an essential source of information. Side-stepping the question of whether these coins were a means of 'propaganda' and whether they were under direct imperial control, it is commonly accepted that central coins at least generally follow imperial wishes (Levick 1999). Changes in the way the emperor was portrayed on coins, then, show how the reality of emperorship (continuous unrest and problems of legitimacy) was reflected in its image. As mentioned above, military qualities had always been an important aspect of imperial representation. *Virtus* (manly courage and military daring) and *providentia* (the foresight required to safeguard the state) together comprised a quarter of all imperial virtues as displayed on *denarii* between AD 69 and 238. *Virtus* alone accounted for 13 per cent. From 238 to 284, however, the number of *virtus* coins struck seems to have risen steeply among the coin types displaying imperial virtues. At the same time, *aequitas* (tranquility, justice), which had constituted 24 per cent from AD 69 to 238, was depicted substantially less often (Noreña 2001: 156; Hekster and Manders 2006). Emperors, then, in their coins as in reality, were judged by different standards.

That also becomes obvious from images on coins of the emperor in a cuirass (**II 47 a; II.48 a**). This type of depiction had a long history, going back to Nero's reign, and had become a common type from the reign of Antoninus Pius (138–61) onwards. In the third century, however, the type becomes dominant, showing, like the increased emphasis on *virtus*, that different qualities were now necessary to become a successful leader. Most strikingly, this is clear from a recent analysis of all centrally minted third-century coin types. These types can be grouped together in thirteen different categories (though some coins cannot be fitted into these), such as, for instance, dynastic or military representation, divine association, emphasis on imperial virtues or the message that the Golden Age was coming about (**II 42**; Manders 2007: 285, 289–90). The military category, referring to the armies, victories, subdued areas, or depicting the emperor as a general or victor, is the single largest group, and comprises over 20 per cent of all coin types. The 'Golden Age' category, which emphasises the peace and prosperity that the emperor will bring about, comprises nearly 20 per cent of coin types. Some 17 per cent stresses the imperial virtues – within which military qualities had risen in status. In the third century, then, approximately every other coin showed the emperor as someone who would bring military glory or peace. In substantial periods of third-century history, the difference would have been hard to tell. Still, the qualities that were stressed on these coins had always been present, and the modes through which they were stressed were familiar ones.

Something similar can be seen when looking at third-century imperial busts (Kleiner 1992: 361–76). Typically, a lot of these, especially in the second half of the century, were characterised by a very short haircut, similar to the one soldiers had (**II 49 d, e**). This was a more military image, often with a short beard instead of the fuller beard that had become standard from Hadrian's portraiture onwards (**II 49 a**). The difference from these earlier Antonine portraits and their elaborate haircuts is clear for all to see. This change, however, took some time in coming. Caracalla (**II 49 b**) was the first to break with tradition, creating an image that has been regularly interpreted as more soldier-like than that of his predecessors, with his shorter beard and frowning look. He may have started the search for a new imperial image. Macrinus (**II 49 c**) hearkened back to the Antonine beard, but combined it with a soldier's crop. Maximinus Thrax (**II.49 d**) unsurprisingly showed himself strong, muscular and soldier-like. This image was further developed in the Capitoline bust of Decius (**II 49 e**). This emperor seems to have been supported by the Senate, which would explain

Eutropius' positive attitude towards him (II 5 9.4). Perhaps encouraged by that support, Decius added 'Trajan' to his own name, associating himself with the 'best of all rulers', as the second-century emperor was commonly considered. Yet notwithstanding this return to tradition, his portrait has the cropped military hairstyle, and a short beard which is similar to Caracalla's. At the same time, this wonderful sculpture, which must have been made by a master artist, shows the emperor as a man with concerns and anxiety, though this may also be in the eye of the beholder. There is always a risk when stylistic arguments are used to describe a ruler's mentality.

Much stronger – though perhaps no clearer – conclusions can be drawn form Gallienus' portraiture. His reign saw (see above, pp. 15–16) some of the worst moments in Roman history. But rather than reacting to this by depicting himself through portraiture which emphasised his military qualities, Gallienus used a wholly different mode of representation. One mode was hearkening back to better times (**II 49 f**). A colossal marble portrait from Greece or Asia Minor, which is dated to approximately AD 267 and is now in the Ny Carlsberg Glyptotek in Copenhagen, bears a marked likeness to Hadrian's portrait. This may be linked to the message of a Golden Age, which was so common on third-century coinage. Rather than emphasising his military status – which after Valerian's imprisonment would look rather shaky – Gallienus referred to happier times that under his leadership would return. On some of his coins the message was, however, more directly related to the military troubles Rome was in at the time. For instance, a coin minted in Rome in AD 263/4 stressed the safety of the world (*securitas orbis*), which Gallienus, depicted in cuirass, had brought (or was about to bring) about (**II 47 a**). But a wholly different mode of representation becomes clear from an earlier marble portrait (c. AD 260–5) which was found in the house of the Vestals in the Forum Romanum (**II 49 g**). Here, the emperor is looking upwards, his idealised features depicting a youthful beauty. Indeed, scholars have interpreted this as a more charismatic depiction of emperorship. This would link nicely with the last large category of imperial coin types: associations with the divine, which seem to have increased in the course of the third century (**II 42**). Indeed, on Gallienus' coins a number of gods are put forward as *conservator Augusti* – placing the emperor under their special protection.

In AD 267/8 there was even an 'animal series', depicting gods with their symbolic animal (de Blois 1976: 160; Weigel 1990). Gods who are so depicted are Diana, Jupiter, Sol and Apollo (**II 47 b**). The latter has as his 'animal' a centaur holding bow and arrow. This may be linked with the centaur Chiron, who was taught archery by Apollo, and taught the latter's son Asclepius medicine in turn.

Confusing as these images might be, they show that there were still alternative representations for emperors to use, even if most rulers depicted themselves in warrior style. The emperors as a group might have been 'soldier emperors', but that need not mean that this was the way in which all emperors presented themselves. Equally important, though there are (notwithstanding the individual differences) marked changes from second- to third-century portraiture, the difference from Tetrarchic images (Rees 2004: 192–6) is far more pronounced still. In the Tetrarchy, perhaps, 'a militarized bureaucracy was the watchword', but many of the soldier emperors of the third century still placed their changed message in a traditional framework. This is exemplified by Philip the Arab, whose forced treaty to buy off the Persians was depicted on his coins as the creation of proper peace. These coins (**II 45 b**) showed the emperor on the obverse with a standard radiate crown, and emphasised through the reverse legend how Philip had guaranteed the safety of the world (*securitas orbis*), much as Gallienus would do later in the face of overwhelming chaos. The coins might have easily have been struck much earlier in the principate. Only those in the know could perhaps read the changed reality between the traditional lines.

The emperor as centre of the world

Changes in the ways emperors managed to get to the throne and changes in the ways they presented themselves are of course important. Yet they need not tell the full story. Military men who temporarily gain their position through civil war and backstabbing do not seem the most obvious points of reference for the many non-military men who lived in the empire to send requests to. Roman emperorship, however, was for a great part defined by responding to exactly these kinds of requests (Millar 1992[2]). Who the emperor was, and how he had gained power, might have been less important than how easily he could be approached by his subjects to settle their differences and solve their daily life problems. Talking about 'soldier emperors' may lead to ignoring this day-to-day functioning of emperorship in the third century.

In fact, responding to requests remained an essential part of emperorship. As supreme ruler, the emperor was the ultimate judge, and was in this capacity approached by a substantial number of his subjects. One should not underestimate their number. For example, in

Severan times, an Egyptian *strategos* named Serapion seems to have heard and answered (though not, one would think, in person) the staggering number of 1,804 cases within three days in March 209 (*P.Yale* I, 61). If anything, the problematic economic situation in different areas of the empire, and the occasional lack of clarity concerning who at local level could still deal with the problems of the lower levels of society (see above, Chapter 2), must have led to more petitions to the emperor. It is perhaps not coincidental that the only inscription giving the whole text of an imperial petition is the already discussed petition from the villagers of Skaptopara to Gordian III in AD 238 (see above, Chapters 1 and 2). The problems – abuse by soldiers and other officials who should have been there to protect their interests – have already been set out above. But the fact that villagers continued to go to the emperor indicates that notwithstanding all the problems and changes in empire and emperorship, the emperor remained, for many, the centre of their world, the supreme point of reference. That does not mean they always got what they wanted. The reaction of Gordian III to the petition from Skaptopara, simply to refer the petitioners back to the governor, was clearly a disappointment. The inscription, as a result, seems to have been put up not by the town to show the emperor's beneficence, but rather by the bearer of the petition, the praetorian soldier Aurelius Pyrrhus, to show the efforts he had undergone for his hometown (Hauken 1998: 82). Ironically, the long and frequent imperial absences from Rome (see above, Chapter 1) may well have boosted the number of petitions. Emperors had always been expected to move through the realm and make themselves visible and approachable to their subjects. The extent to which this mobility was taken in the third century may have been unwelcome to Rome, but it did make it easier for provincial subjects to present petitions to the emperor, and certainly stimulated them to do so (Fowler and Hekster 2005: 13; Hauken 1998: 151; Birley 1988: 138). The emperor remained central to the realm, even when Rome became less so.

Requests by individuals are not the only way through which the continuous – or perhaps even increasing – centrality of third-century emperorship becomes clear. Cities as a whole, too, acclaimed and made requests to rulers. In fact, from the late second century onwards such acclamations were more and more often recorded verbatim in inscriptions including, from the reign of Caracalla onwards, inscriptions on milestones. At the same time, cities started to issue coins with acclamations of emperors on the reverses (Roueché 1984: 185–6). This increasing tendency to record acclamations shows how it had become more important to show public approval to the powers that be, a development which was eventually recognised by Constantine, who encouraged provincials to praise (and blame!) officials by acclamation. These acclamations were then reported to the emperor himself (*CTh* 1.16.6). Passing a decree to congratulate new emperors also showed the cities' allegiance, and this was much appreciated, as imperial responses to decrees from the city of Aphrodisias make clear (**II 24 20**; Reynolds 1982: 131–3). Gordian III in AD 239 (the second year of his tribunician power) responded favourably to a message which the Aphrodisians went to some length to get to the emperor. They sent a certain Claudius Hegemoneus to the emperor to make sure that the latter was aware that they had passed a decree of congratulations. The emperor, in turn, explicitly praises the townsmen for their behaviour, and confirms all their rights. A very similar event took place eleven years later when, at the start of the joint reign of Trajan Decius and his son Herennius Etruscus, two ambassadors who are not otherwise known were sent to the emperors to inform them that Aphrodisias had marked the beginning of their rule with a decree of congratulations (**II 24 25**; Reynolds 1982: 140–3). Again confirmation of all its rights, and even a promise of future goodwill, are the result. Both letters were included amongst the inscriptions in the so-called 'archive wall' in the theatre of Aphrodisias – clear for all to see. Positive imperial reactions to the praise of towns was not new, and there had been embassies going to the emperors to express gladness at their accession (and so retain good standing) from the beginning of the imperial era (Millar 1992[2]: 410–20). Yet in the third century, with its rapid turnover of emperors, there were risks in too readily greeting an emperor. Aphrodisias, as it turns out, did well, but in the aftermath of the year AD 238 (see above, p. 14) there may well have been some who felt that officially congratulating Gordian III might not have been the safest course of action.

A safer way in which a town could request maintenance of its standing, or ask for further privileges, was to accommodate imperial wishes, as many towns seem to have done when Caracalla wanted to be crowned for his many 'victories' (**II 1 78.9.2**). Alternatively, cities could acclaim the emperor at a later stage. This seems to have been the case in the instance of the longest acclamation inscribed on a single stone, from Perge in Pamphylia during the brief reign of Tacitus (AD 275–6) (**II 25**), which has been analysed expertly by Charlotte Roueché. The acclamation seems to coincide with the bestowal by Tacitus of the title 'Metropolis of Pamphylia' on the city, which was also celebrated on local coinage. This acclamation was probably recorded at a gathering of townspeople, and may well have been a copy of a document sent to the emperor (Roueché 1989: 208). Imperial power may have changed in the third century, but in the fierce inter-town competition, imperial approval was still of utmost importance. The emperor remained the central figure who could bestow honour in a way nobody else could. The honours which Perge chose to mention are also interesting, and can sometimes be contested. For instance, the town of Side, the most important neighbour of Perge, also had right of asylum and also claimed to be the crown of Pamphylia – its most important city. Being 'Metropolis of Pamphylia' may have given Perge the upper hand in this. The penultimate line of the acclamation may be a reaction to that claim, or to Side's assertion to be a six-time *neokoros*, having been given the right to built a temple to the imperial cult six times, outranking Perge's four (see below, p. 65). Perge also links itself to the emperor by being the assize centre, and (possibly) the place where the provincial officer of the imperial *fiscus* resides (Roueché 1989: 209–15). Finally, it is noteworthy that, though the acclamation is in Greek, the goddesses who are mentioned are referred to by their Latin name 'Diana' – again stressing Perge's strong Roman links. Again, being Roman remained important even when Rome lost its uncontested superior position.

This Roman-ness was also boosted by the *Constitutio Antoniniana* (**II 20**). Its importance for Roman law and citizenship has been extensively discussed in the previous chapter. But universal citizenship also had repercussions for the position of the emperor. All citizens were now bound by Roman law, which had become universal. Also, as we have seen, most new citizens had somehow become the emperor's namesakes by including his name in their own. Even if Dio's claim that the *Constitutio* was mainly a means to get more taxes was right, the ideological aspects ought not to be forgotten. Caracalla explicitly wanted to include all of his subjects in what he presented as the preservation of his safety. In this way, then, all citizens became linked to the figure of the emperor, for whose well-being they were led 'to the sanctuaries of the gods'. The welfare of the emperor had become central to all his subjects (Potter 2004: 138–9).

Worshipping the emperor

In the course of the third century there seems to have been an increased military presentation of emperorship (though within a traditional framework). At the same time, the figure of the emperor became increasingly important to more subjects, most of them in the provinces.

Yet few, if any, emperors had full control over what happened in the empire. This difference can hardly be better illustrated than by the case of Domitian II. This third-century usurper ruled around AD 271 for such a short period of time and over such a small area of territory that the only traces left of him were some passing comments in the *Historia Augusta* (**II 3a 2.6**). His emperorship was properly confirmed only in 2003, when a bronze coin was found at Chipping Norton, near Oxford, depicting Domitian as emperor on the obverse and proclaiming *Concordia militum* ('harmony of the soldiers') on the reverse (**II 48 c**). This was the second bronze coin which was found of Domitian II's, but the first had been deemed a forgery and was discarded as evidence (Abdy 2004). The example shows how scholars are occasionally too prudent, rejecting ancient statements which end up being true. Equally important, it shows that in the second half of the third century, there really were an extraordinary number of usurpers with a certain measure of success. One might even argue that the many usurpers further suggest the importance of the emperor in the third century as an ultimate focal point. All local zones wanted to have their own Roman emperor whom they could refer to. The many third-century 'local heroes' were obvious candidates. These, however, could only present themselves one-dimensionally since they simply did not have the time to do otherwise. None of them, therefore, could really impose themselves upon the empire. Still, the sheer number of such usurpers influenced the popular perception of emperorship and must have made the limits of imperial power clear.

One way of bridging the gap between a reality in which the emperors had only limited control over their realm and an image in which they were central to every aspect of its functioning was turning to the divine. This was not new. From the beginning, Roman emperorship had held divine connotations. Throughout the empire, people built altars and temples to the emperors and offered them supreme worship. Nor was this a small-scale phenomenon, with over 150 imperial temples and shrines catalogued for Asia Minor alone (Price 1984). The geographical diversification was such that one cannot speak of *the* imperial cult, but should speak instead of imperial cults. In these cults, worship of the emperor was often placed within local religious traditions (Beard et al. 1998: 348–52, 360). This practice continued in the third century, as did the competition between towns about who was most faithful to the emperor. The latter is clear from the emphasis a town like Perge places on being four times *neokoros* (**II 25**). To an extent, however, the increased centrality of emperorship in combination with a diminished reputation of individual emperors would change the system. Increasingly, the emperor would be linked to a specific god, the choice of which could depend on the emperor's personal religious notions. For instance, the emperor Elagabalus worshipped the eponymous chief deity from his home town Emesa in the shape of a black stone (**II 43 a, b; II 5 8.22**). He explicitly presented himself as high priest and servant of a powerful god who would strengthen his position. The emperor was in this way linked to the god who was presented as the new chief deity of the empire (Icks 2006). This behaviour was exceptional and much commented upon even in the early third century, but in previous times it would have been unthinkable. Furthermore, it was not so different from the later behaviour of Aurelian, who in AD 274 held his triumph for bringing the empire together again, and then dedicated a splendid temple to the sun god, which he filled with treasure (**II 5 9.15**; Gradel 2002: 351–2). In the same year, he also depicted Sol on his coins, linked to his victories in the East (**II 48 a**). Oriens was part of the empire again, thanks to an emperor who is shown in military gear, and the sun god who helped him achieve this (Watson 1999: 183–96). This was one step in the trajectory that would lead to worship, not of the emperor as such, but of the emperor as a servant of an ever higher supreme being.

Another crucial aspect of emperor worship, and for the perception of emperorship as a whole, was the worship of *divi*, emperors who had been deified after their deaths. The importance that those *divi* had in Roman daily life becomes clear from the so called *Feriale Duranum* (**II.26**; and see below, Chapter 5). This is a religious calendar from the reign of Severus Alexander, found amongst papyri belonging to an auxiliary cohort which was based at Dura Europos, a town on the Euphrates, the furthest eastern frontier of the empire. It is noticeable how numerically dominant the sacrifices for the divine emperors and indeed empresses are, though the latter only received public prayer, as opposed to an ox for the emperor. Sacrificing an ox was expensive – especially in times of economic constraints – but this seems not to have hampered sacrifices to the *divi*. A beautiful and extremely important description of how the apotheosis of an emperor worked at his funeral can be found in the works of Herodian. He describes the burial of Septimius Severus (**II 2 4.2**), an occasion he was most probably present at. With the accounts of the apotheosis of Augustus and Pertinax, it is one of only three such descriptions (Zanker 2004). Herodian's text stresses the tripartite division in the period between the emperor's death and his deification. In the first stage, a wax pendant of the emperor's body was displayed on the Palatine from the emperor's death up to the day of his funeral. This body double would be treated as if it were a patient, allowing for ritual festivities (and doubtless for people from far afield to come to Rome). Then, in the second stage of the ritual, the body double is taken in procession first to the Forum Romanum and then to his pyre on the Campus Martius – with, as we know from other texts, representatives of the whole of the Roman world forming part of the pomp. The third and final stage, as recounted by Herodian, sees the wax body placed in the pyre, and set alight. This set in process the presumed transformation from human emperor to immortal god – symbolised by an eagle which flew up from the pyre.

It is remarkable how similar the description of Severus' deification is to those of Augustus and Pertinax. Herodian, however, omits one noticeable fact: the decision to deify fell to the senate, who could thus give honour to worthwhile rulers. Notwithstanding the similarities between Augustus' and Severus' apotheoses, there was a clear difference as well. Whereas with Augustus this system of deification was new, by the third century there were already a great many *divi* who were worshipped. Twenty are mentioned in the acts of the Arval Brethren – a priestly college in Rome – in AD 224, and that number probably excludes some of the members of the imperial household who had simply received the title *divus* or *diva*, as opposed to the ones who received a temple and priests as well (Gradel 2002: 355–6). In the further course of the third century, then:

> Doubts about the system of deification must have been aggravated by the steadily increasing number of *Divi*, gods of little or no power. The decreasing influence of the Roman Senate, whose role and function was of decisive importance to the didactic point of deifying dead emperor and empresses, must have added even more pressure. (Gradel 2002: 356)

It may, in this light, be telling that the last emperor to receive his own state temple was Marcus Aurelius, and that from AD 180 onwards there were few temples constructed to the goddess Roma and the deified emperors. There is perhaps even some evidence that shortly after the *Feriale Duranum* was composed, the worship of *divi* suffered a severe setback. In Herodian's fierce attack on Maximinus Thrax (II 2 7.3.5) he mentions how this ruler took as much money as he could, not even sparing temples and the statues of the gods. This may have been sacrilege, but it did not hamper cult activities. The *divi*, on the other hand, were robbed of their 'honours', which in this context usually means cult activities. Apparently Herodian means to say that Maximinus took the temple funds or discontinued the cults as a whole

(Gradel 2002: 357). Even if the situation was not quite so drastic, the fact that cults of the deified emperors are singled out in Herodian's account means that they had lost status in comparison with the cults of 'ordinary gods'. A short statement in the *Historia Augusta* describes how the emperor Tacitus – who was senatorially chosen and thus approved of by the unknown author of the text – built a temple to the deified emperors of undisputed reputation (**II 3b 9.5**; see above, Chapter 1) so that they could be worshipped on their birthday, the birthday of the city (the Parilia, 21 April), and when vows were taken for the emperor's health on 3 January. The construction of such a temple makes sense only if the original temples in which these 'good' *divi* were worshipped had closed sometime before (Gradel 2002: 363).

The deified emperors had, however, already returned to the centre of attention, if only briefly, during the reign of Trajan Decius. He issued coins depicting all male *divi*. On these coins obvious good examples like Augustus and Decius' new namesake Trajan (see above, p. 60) were shown (**II 46 a, b**) but also more disputed rulers like Commodus (**II 46 c**). The series ends with the divine Severus Alexander (**II 46 d**). All coins show on the obverse the image of the *divus*. The legend reads: 'to the deified Augustus/Trajan/Commodus/Alexander'. On the reverse, they show that these are consecration coins, stating so explicitly, and depicting a lighted rectangular altar. The emperors of old were important again. This return to a traditional worship of the deified emperors was combined with an edict ordering that all inhabitants of the empire had to sacrifice to the traditional Roman gods – an edict that would give rise to the first persecution of Christians. This, however, can only be understood within the wider context of religious developments, as will be addressed in the following chapter.

CHAPTER 5

Christianity and Religious Change

There is hardly a subject in third-century history which has been debated more frequently and more intensively than that of centrally organised Christian persecutions. Christianity is, even more than Roman law, the most instantly recognisable inheritance from the Roman Empire. Persecution and martyrdom, furthermore, have been a near constant part of Christian history. Christians were often persecuted by others: Romans of course, and Persians, but as late as 850 there were also martyrs in then-Muslim Cordova. In addition, Christians have persecuted other Christians whom they regarded as heretics, from at least the Constantinian age onwards.

> As a result, the ideal of martyrdom has remained alive in world history, since its first formulations by Jews in mid-second century BC. Christianity has never lost it, and it was probably through contact with Christians, not Jews, that early Islam picked up its analogous language and theology for those who die for the faith. The legacy is still tragically fresh. (Lane Fox 1986: 420)

This claim, from an important analysis of the relationship between Christianity and paganism, now holds more true than ever. Recent years have once again made clear how fundamentally the notion of martyrdom can impact on world history. The Christian notion of martyrdom was much developed during the third century, when, for the first time, persecutions became centrally organised. At the same time Christianity had always been a problematic religion for Rome. Being Christian made it impossible to take part in Rome's public sacrifices, which placed Christians on the wrong side of social custom, if not the law. That did not mean they were persecuted. Famously, in an exchange with Pliny, the emperor Trajan (II 27) had stated that acknowledged Christians who did not repent should be prosecuted, but not searched

69

out. Before AD 249, there had been occasions on which Christians were killed for their belief, but these had been local affairs, like the executions in the arena of Christians at Lugdunum during the reign of Marcus Aurelius (Birley 1987: 202–4). At a local level matters went awry, and individuals sought a party responsible for the disturbance of divine support. Christians were obvious candidates (Clarke 2005: 616). This would change dramatically with Decius' decree about a universal sacrifice to the gods of the empire in AD 249, paving the way for centrally organised persecutions (de Ste Croix 1963).

Decius' decree: purpose and consequences

The edict of Trajan Decius obliged all inhabitants of the Roman Empire to sacrifice to the gods. Though the text itself has not survived, much can be surmised from other sources, such as the so-called *libelli* (**II 28**). These are certificates following a fairly consistent format. They state that individuals (amongst whom are many with the name Aurelius; see above, Chapter 3) performed sacrifices before officers, and are dated exactly and signed by witnesses. The sacrificers also testify to their loyalty to the gods by swearing that they have been zealous in sacrificing before. All inhabitants of the empire seem to have had to do so on a specified day, much as in the system of census registration or tax collection (Rives 1999: 149). Forty-four of these *libelli* have been found so far, and their consistency in format seems to imply that they were prescribed within Decius' edict (Knipfing 1923; Rives 1999: 135–6). Also, there are the writings of Cyprian (see above, Chapter 2), who was bishop of Carthage at the time but went into hiding during the persecutions which followed Decius' edict, and of the Alexandrian bishop Dionysios, preserved through quotations of the church historian Eusebius, who was born just after the event. As often, the Thirteenth Sibylline Oracle provides (somewhat minimal) clues (**II 9 81–8**). Describing the reign of Trajan Decius, it refers to the emperor's Dacian descent (though he was actually born in Pannonia) and his assuming of the name 'Trajan' (T = 300). It places Decius in the fourth race, which could either imply the fourth kingdom before world's end, as in the biblical vision of Daniel (Daniel 7) or the Hesiodic Race of Iron. It explicitly states that 'the faithful' (the Christians) are killed, and gives as reason 'the former king'. This might refer to Philip the Arab's alleged – almost certainly apocryphal – Christianity, which would make Decius' order specifically aimed at Christians, in order to distance himself from his predecessor (Potter 1990: 258–68). The latter point cannot be of real importance (and is most likely simply wrong), but on the question of whether the purpose of the edict was specifically anti-Christian, there is substantial debate.

That the edict making sacrifice obligatory, and checking this administratively, had terrible consequences for Christians in the Roman Empire is beyond doubt. Whereas before Christians had been at worst local scapegoats, they would now suffer the explicit disapproval of the imperial court. Decius, as discussed at the end of the previous chapter, gave renewed attention to the deified emperors. He is also honoured as *restitutor sacrorum*, 'restorer of sacred matters', which probably refers to rites (*AE* 1973. 235). It may well have been that in times of difficulty, he was making a concerted effort to guarantee divine support. The millennium festivities (delayed to AD 248), or more specifically the worries that the passing of a millennium can cause, may have played a part in this (**II 5 9.3**; Potter 2004: 243). Minds needed to be put at ease. Yet Christians could not act accordingly. They would not sacrifice to the (unspecified) gods, and were thus openly opposing the emperor. They were sought out, put on trial, and – unless they renounced their faith – suffered the consequences. Many were imprisoned, tortured and killed (Clarke 2005: 632–5).

That does not mean it was Decius' explicit aim to act against Christians. Two recent expert analyses of the events take diametrically opposed views. On the one hand, it is argued that Decius' decree shows above all the increase of central power as described in previous chapters. Christianity suffered as a side-effect:

> About Decius' edict there is, however, a foretaste of that autocracy which marks fourth-century government: directives are being issued from above affecting the lives of the entire empire as the central authorities attempt to grapple with the problems of commanding and controlling an unwieldy and extremely diverse empire. There is here a presage of those centralist pressures for conformity and homogeneity ... But it is clear that an attack on Christianity as such was not the object of the legislation. (Clarke 2005: 626)

Only when Christians refused to conform were they 'persuaded' to comply, with the death penalty only sometimes the ultimate consequence.

This view is not shared by all, however:

> It is debated whether [Decius'] order was from the outset targeted against the Christians, or whether it was simply the refusal of (some) Christians to comply which unleashed persecution on them. The latter view seems oddly

academic to me: no emperor or his administration in the mid-third century could have been so utterly uninformed as to be unaware that Christians, or some of them, would be the only substantial group of the empire who would either refuse to comply or betray their beliefs (Jews were specifically exempt from the order). So I take it as obvious that the original edict was indeed from the outset targeted against Christians, though they were not mentioned in it. (Gradel 2002: 368)

In this second view, then, isolating a group of 'outsiders' would guarantee a return to the support that the gods had given Rome before. Eradicating Christians would bring back the *pax deorum*.

However contradictory these two views may seem, in both cases the main purpose of the edict is a return to better times by pleasing the gods. Alternatively, Decius' main reason for the edict may have had more to do with his own rather weak position as emperor in times of near-continuous usurpation, himself a usurper who had betrayed his emperor. By making everyone sacrifice to the Roman gods including the emperor, Decius guaranteed loyalty. The motives behind the decree, in this reading, are somewhat similar to one of Caracalla's reasons for the *Constitutio Antoniniana* (see above, Chapter 3) (Potter 2004: 241–3; Bleckmann 2006). Whatever the motive, the decree was extraordinary, perhaps a reflection of extraordinary times. Still, as with the *Constitutio Antoniniana*, no 'true' objective can be stated and a combination of motives should be kept in mind. Perhaps Decius even put less thought into issuing the decree than modern scholars have into finding the reasons why he did so (Rives 1999: 151).

The consequences of Decius' orders are less disputed. First, it strengthened those who had worried about Christians in the belief that they were to blame for all that went wrong in the world, which was one cause of the persecutions. It may not be coincidental that shortly after Decius' death, when it turned out that his successor Gallus did not continue the edict, Cyprian wrote his famous address to Demetrianus. In it, Cyprian refutes a pagan who blames Christians for all the famine, war and illness that plagued parts of the Roman world (see above, Chapter 2). The fact that Christians do not worship pagan gods is explicitly mentioned (**II 29 3**). One reason that Cyprian has to offer for the evils in the world is that it is simply growing old (**II 29 3–4**), but he goes further (**II 29 5**); the true reason is that pagans do not worship the Christian god. Clearly, the complaints about Christian non-sacrifice needed answering. At the same time, the tone Cyprian chooses is not cowering. On the contrary, he explicitly holds paganism to blame for what befalls men – the revenge of God. Perhaps this was also to convince wavering Christians of the rightness of their belief, and what the wrath of God could be like. Christians will have wavered even more during persecutions, since part of Trajan's advice to Pliny (**II 27**) still held. If a Christian repented and denied the Christian god, all was forgiven. This, in fact, gave rise to a second consequence of Decius' edict. Many chose to live rather than to remain faithful. Afterwards churches had to deal with readmitting the fallen. A long legacy of disputes and bitterness within the Christian communities followed the end of Decius' persecutions (Clarke 2005: 635). That, perhaps, explains the bitter tone of Cyprian – who also gave a sermon 'On the lapsed' – in his address on the 'practicalities' of the trials.

In this sermon (**II 29 13**) the difference between a religion of ritual and a religion of belief comes eloquently to the fore (Price 1984: 9–15). Cyprian does not understand – or in a playful argument purports not to understand – why concealing true belief should guarantee freedom from persecution. Concealing the true belief in Christianity ought to be punished, he argues, not encouraged. Of course such concealment would in practice mean sacrifice, and thus conformity to ritual tradition. In fact, Roman officials often sought for modes of sacrifice that would be acceptable to Christians, and were astonished at what could only be interpreted as supreme (and illogical) stubbornness (Lane Fox 1986: 421). Cyprian (**II 29 13**) describes a Christian who heroically defies Rome publicly, stays true and is only punished in the flesh, and mockingly asks Rome the question why public denial makes the crime worse; a question the relevance of which many Romans could not have understood. Yet the number of martyrs was always only a fraction of those who lapsed, or, like Cyprian during Decius' persecutions, simply hid. Perhaps some of Cyprian's tone was overcompensation for his own not exemplary behaviour – though he would die a martyr's death in the end. A third consequence of the measure was recently recognised in a splendid article on Decius' decree (Rives 1999: 152): by making participation in a centrally proclaimed cultic act obligatory for all inhabitants of the Roman Empire, the decree paved the way for what could be called 'the religion of the Roman Empire', as opposed to the variety of local religions which had up to then defined the religious framework. This was not centred on the emperor, since imperial cult was at best of secondary importance in the persecutions (Millar 1973). Nor was it, yet, centred on a particular deity. It was defined by sacrifice. Ultimately, the religion of the empire would turn out to be Christianity. Ironically, the first steps towards this also created the framework for persecutions.

Christian persecutions and their context

Decius' decree may have affected Christians only as a side-effect. Under the emperor Valerian, Christians were targeted explicitly. Again, Cyprian is an important source, though this time the bishop would not survive the persecution. Apparently (and in the face of the problems the empire was facing, understandably) under Valerian there was renewed stress on homogeneous worship of the gods who guaranteed the security of Rome. Christians seem to have replied that they already prayed for the well-being of empire and emperor. This was not acceptable. Whatever the precise circumstances, in AD 257 Valerian forbade Christian gatherings and entering of their cemeteries. Christians had to conform to Rome. The higher clergy were to be arrested and had to sacrifice. If they did not, they were to suffer the consequences. Unclear about what these consequences were, the senate asked Valerian what to do with those who disobeyed (Potter 2004: 255; Clarke 2005: 637–42). Valerian's response left no room for doubt. We know of it from a letter of Cyprian to his fellow bishop Successus (II 30), his 'brother' within the Christian family, from AD 258. Clearly, Christians had been aware for some time of rumours about anti-Christian events: being 'under threat of the arena' clearly referred to a martyr's death. Cyprian sent men to Rome to find out, showing the Christian information network that had developed following the Decian troubles, as is also clear from the last paragraph, in which Cyprian asks Successus to spread the news (Alföldy 1973: 481–2). These men heard Valerian's answer to the senatorial question. Leading Christians should be executed, unless they were men of high standing. Even these would have only temporary respite before suffering the death penalty. Women, too, were targeted, even those connected to 'Caesar's household', meaning those working at the imperial court (including slaves and freedwomen). They were sent to imperial estates – here meaning the mines, from which few if any came back alive.

This imperial reaction was made known to governors of the provinces, leaving them no alternative but to start arresting Christian clergy. How serious the consequences would be is also clear from Cyprian's writing: Xistus, that is, pope Sixtus II, was martyred in Rome at the cemetery of St Callistus alongside four deacons. Cyprian himself would be martyred shortly afterwards. Many martyrs would follow, although, in reading the sources, one should always keep in mind that only a minority volunteered to die. Theirs, however, were the stories that were seen as heroic by the 'fallen' and overlooked. These latter groups celebrated and took courage from the accounts of the martyrs (Lane Fox 1986: 444–5). Valerian had written his response to the Senate from outside Rome (**II 30**). In AD 258 he was already in the East, where he would suffer his great defeat. Shortly afterwards, the Palmyrene and Gallic Empires would show how fragmented the Roman Empire was becoming (see above, Chapter 1). Perhaps Gallienus realised that this was no time for internal division, and he issued an edict of restitution (de Blois 1976: 177–85), which was celebrated as a victory for the Christian god by later Christian authors. As it was, there would be more – and much more intensive – persecutions later, but these were to take place in the Tetrarchic age, and should be seen in context (Rees 2004: 66–71).

For emperors, and indeed for local communities, Christians were a problem because they would not sacrifice on behalf of the empire. Roman polytheists could not understand the exclusivity of Christian worship. For Christians, at the same time, this exclusivity was the root of their religion. Cyprian makes this clear, for instance in his above-discussed address to Demetrianus. Those who do not worship the true god cannot know the truth (**II 29 3**). Indeed, for Cyprian, the pagan inability to understand that there is only one god is at the root of the problems in the world (**II 29 5**). In a passage that must have been nothing short of offensive to a Roman readership, free citizens are even compared to slaves, showing how omnipotent the Christian god is (**II.29 8**). For third-century Christians, the end of the world was nigh, it could even come in their own lifetime (**II.29 5, 9**). The latter notion was debatable; Cyprian in his writing shows a development from thinking that Judgement Day was about to come to the view that the world would continue for a while after all (Alföldy 1973: 482–90). But even if the Empire of God had not yet arrived, it was the soul that was important. Punishment of the flesh was as nothing compared to sins of the souls (**II 29 9, 13**).

The importance of purity of the soul, in combination with the inspiration which lapsed Christians could take from the accounts of heroic deaths, explains the importance of the martyr account for the development of early Christianity. Some even stated that provoking the authorities into acting, becoming a voluntary martyr, was the best way to honour god (de Ste Croix 1963). Martyrs' accounts could become very popular, as is shown by perhaps the most important of these texts, the *Passion of Perpetua and Felicitas* (**II 31**). The popularity of the text was such that it was still read often in church towards the end of the fourth century, though it was written as part of the Montanist movement in Christianity, which had by that time been declared heretical (Shaw 1993: 37–41; Grig 2004; Butler 2006). Perpetua was a well-born and married twenty-two-year-old Christian, who was martyred as early as AD 203. Alongside her, the slave-girl Felicitas was arrested, as well as their teacher Saturus. The text consists of a narrative framework which includes apparently first-hand accounts. These accounts seem in fact to be actual contemporary texts. If, as seems likely, the story by Perpetua was written by her, and possibly later taken from her diary (**II 31 14**) it would be the oldest surviving text by a Christian woman. It also gives us supreme insight into her and her co-martyrs' religious experiences and into the way Romans punished Christians. However, the description of the martyrs' deaths is the least trustworthy part of the *Passion*, filled with improbabilities, possibly catering to the tastes of the times (Bremmer 2004). Some aspects are worth pointing out all the same.

The martyrs' deaths were gruesome, which the passion makes explicit. The Christians were tortured but stayed calm under abuse (**II 31 16**), even if they had to succumb to animals in the amphitheatre, or were executed there in full public view (**II 31 20–1**). The horrors were recounted, but the martyrs did not suffer. Even when the girls Perpetua and Felicitas had to suffer bestiality (**II 31 20**), the emphasis is on how they maintained their modesty, and were so much in the Spirit that they did not suffer. Likewise, their companion Saturus preserved ultimate composure whilst dying (**II 31 21**), giving hope to those surrounding him. The quantity of blood he lost shows how horrid his death was, but this too is seen in religious terms, as a second baptism. The horrors of violence are placed against the serenity brought by belief (Lane Fox 1986: 438–9). More insight into these martyrs' psyche is granted by the description of several of their dreams and visions (**II 31 10–11**). Suffering of the flesh and dying in the arena was interpreted by Perpetua as a fight with the devil, wherein she would be victorious (**II 31 10**). Saturus, in his vision, describes the paradise which they would reach after dying. In fact, in his vision he meets other Christian martyrs, including Saturninus, who had been arrested at the same time as they were (Bremmer 2003; Shaw 1993). The martyrs were certain of their spiritual superiority, as long as they relinquished earthly bounds. Martyrdom brought the glory of god, as is clear from the haunting account of Felicitas' distress that – due to her pregnancy – her punishment might be postponed (**II 31 15**). She prayed to go into labour so that she could be executed punctually, and her wish was granted. A guard who mocked Felicitas' pain in childbirth was reminded that at her execution it was God who would take her suffering, not she. Nor did the daughter who was born tie Felicitas down; she was instantly given away to a sister. This was what many in early Christianity saw as exemplary behaviour. Small wonder that Romans had difficulty comprehending Christianity.

Other Christians took a somewhat different view from voluntary martyrs, and rather tried to tie Christianity into ancient traditions with which pagan Romans were familiar. How this could be done is evident from Marcus Minucius Felix's *Octavius* (II 32). This is one of the earliest surviving apologies by a converted Roman and describes a discussion between two of Minucius Felix's friends, the eponymous Christian Octavius Januarius and the pagan Caecilius Natalis. Octavius tries to argue at length (II 32 21.1–4) how within paganism the notion of man-turned-god is engrained – countering the argument that Christ would be weak because he was a man, going back to the likes of Euhemerus (who argued that gods were excellent kings of the past). Octavius also brings in a famous anecdote about a letter which was written by Alexander the Great to his mother, discussing secrets told to him when he visited the temple of Ammon in Egypt. The letter, allegedly, discussed first Vulcan and later Jupiter and his family. It then discussed the myth of Isis and Osiris (II 32 21.3). This mythological account told how, holding castanets, Isis sought out the pieces of the body of her husband and brother Osiris, who flew round his grave in the shape of a swallow. All of these stories, Octavius argues, show how the pagan gods were human in origin. Yet even in such a text, the glory of spiritual victory is emphasised (II 32 37.1) in tones similar to that of the passions. And here too, notions of sacrifice had to be addressed (II 32 38.1). The latter was to respond to Caecilius' objections on the subject (II 32 12.5). These objections, of course, were also written down by the Christian Minucius Felix. The disdain for Jews (II 32 10.4) may have more to do with Christian antagonism towards the religion from which Christianity obviously descended than with showing pagan sentiments. On the whole, Rome had few objections to Judaism, of which they recognised the ancientness – as long as Jews did not rebel against Rome. Yet in order to work as the apologetic text that it is, the pagan objections needed to relate to reality. Not surprisingly, then, the argument about the existence of the Roman gods (II 32 8.1) and the supremacy they have brought Rome (II 32 12.5) are placed at the beginning of Caecilius' argument. Before Christianity, Rome had been gloriously protected by the gods – when things were going wrong, it made sense to blame Christians.

Continuity and change in third-century religion

Christianity did not start in the third century, and some of the above-sketched problems had already come to the fore much earlier. Until the end of the second century, however, there had been only relatively few Christians, possibly c. 200,000 in AD 200, or less than 0.5 per cent of the total population of the empire (Hopkins 1998). This number grew immensely in the third century, making the 'outsider' status of Christians more prominent, and therefore more problematic. Yet Christians were not the only outsiders. The third century saw also the rise of Manichaeism, a sect that was welcomed by Shapur I and spread into the Roman world, from which it would be banished (without much result) by Diocletian as a new and foreign cult in a famous edict, the text of which has survived (Rees 2004: 174–5).

Mani was born in April 216, near the Sassanian capital Ctesiphon, son of a father who had been converted by a very missionising form of Jewish Christianity, near-extinguished in the Roman world by the formation of a more coherent 'orthodox' Christian doctrine. He was believed to have had visions at twelve and twenty-four years old; after the latter he left the sect of which he was part, and went his own way (Gardner and Lieu 2004: 3–5). The religious system that he ultimately came to promote is a form of 'religious dualism'; all is focused on the two eternal principles of good and evil. Manicheism was a universal faith. Believers had it as their duty to convert others all over the world, so that the new faith would replace other religions, which Mani believed to be corrupt (Frye 2005: 475–6). Travelling wildly during his lifetime, Mani visited much of the Persian Empire and even went as far east as India. He seems not to have travelled into Roman territory himself, but sent missionaries to spread his word instead (Henrichs and Koening 1982: 1–3). The latter point shows that notwithstanding all frontier battles, there was still freedom of movement across the borders between the Roman and Persian Empires.

> Manichaeism expanded rapidly. Partly this must have been the result of its adaptability to the religious environment in which it sought converts. Generally speaking Manichean missionaries were prone to adopt features of Christianity in the West, Zoroastrianism in Iran and Buddhism in the farther east, but claiming that the other religions were incomplete and had become corrupt from the time of their founders. (Frye 2005: 475)

He managed to convert Shapur I (which partly explains the ease with which he and his supporters travelled in the Persian Empire), but was eventually executed in AD 276 by Vahram, the new Persian king. His death did not stop his religion. Indeed, in the West it would remain prominent for a long time, with St Augustine as one of its most well-known adherents and, after his conversion to Christianity, most eloquent opponents. In the East, it survived even longer, existing in China until the early seventeenth century and possibly later (Lane Fox 1986: 562–3; Lieu 1985: 219). For Christianity, Manichaeism was a dangerous rival. That much is also clear from a late third-century papyrus, written by an Egyptian bishop (II 33). Again and again the text warns against the danger of Manichees: they tell lies and are filled with madness. Interestingly, with its emphasis on an exaggerated gruesomeness of Manichaeic ritual, this bishop treats Manichees in much the same way as Christians were treated by others.

The rise of Manichaeism has often been seen as part of a phenomenon in the late second and third century that has been discussed almost as much as Christianity: the rise of so-called oriental religions. Alongside the rise of Manichaeism, the late second and third centuries also saw an increase in the popularity of Mithraism, which like Manichaeism was linked to the Persians. Though much debated, it seems clear that this link was not a direct one. Roman Mithraism was not the final result of a continuous adaptation of its eastern counterpart, but a reinvention (possibly in the first century AD) of this eastern religion in Roman terms (Beck 1998: 122–5). All the same, such a reinvention needs to be explained, as does the simultaneous increase in the popularity of the (eastern) mystery cults of Isis and Magna Mater (the Great Mother). These were cults into which one needed to be initiated, cults that were a form of personal religion (Burkert 1987: 12–29).

Famously, the rise of oriental cults was accounted for by the great Belgian scholar of ancient religions, Franz Cumont. He argued that:

In order to gain the masses and the cream of Roman society (as they did for a whole century) the barbarian mysteries had to possess a powerful charm, they had to satisfy the deep wants of the human soul, and their strength had to be superior to that of the ancient Greco-Roman religion. To explain the reasons for their victory we must try to reveal the nature of this superiority – I mean their superiority in the struggle, without assuming innate superiority. I believe that we can define it by stating that those religions gave greater satisfaction first, to the senses and passions, secondly, to the intelligence, finally, and above all, to the conscience. (Cumont 1911: 28)

Cumont's thesis was that oriental cults filled a void, and under their influence paganism would change, paving the way for Christianity.

The 'sleeping monotheism' in the oriental religions made these cults attractive in what has often been deemed a religious 'age of anxiety' (Dodds 1965). The problems which the Roman Empire faced made people lose faith, and alternatives were sought to Rome's traditional gods. Famously, the Neoplatonist philosopher Plotinus, whose writing ranks amongst the most important works of this period, joined Gordian III in his expedition against the Persians (see above, p. 19) to make contact with philosophers from Persia and India, and so learn eastern thinking.

Still, the story cannot have been so straightforward. Apart from (possibly) Mithraism, mystery cults did not offer the idea of personal spiritual progress (Gordon 1994: 465–7). Nor should the rise of the orient be exaggerated. In the third century, the vast majority of evidence for worship concerns the traditional Roman gods, especially Jupiter Optimus Maximus. Inscriptions testify that if there was a diminished confidence in traditional gods, it did not affect the worship of those very deities. Only in less than 10 per cent of cases did inscriptions refer to oriental deities, like the ones named above, or the Syrian Jupiter Dolichenus (Alföldy 1989: 373–81). The rise of the east was limited; apart from the imperial support for Elagabalus (see above, p. 66), there is little evidence that support for oriental cults was encouraged by emperors. Speculations that link Aurelian's Sol Invictus (see above, Chapter 4) to the Palmyrene deities Bel and Yarhibol are ultimately unconvincing (Watson 1999: 195–6; Kaizer 2002: 154–7). Aurelian's combination on coins of Sol and the Oriens (**II 48 a**; and see above, p. 66) celebrated the emperor's victory in the east, not the victory of an eastern god.

Of course, this is not to deny any change. But Roman religion was famously inclusive. Gods, cults and whole religions could exist alongside one another. Religion in the Roman world can be characterised as 'religious pluralism', though there does seem to have been a second- and third-century development towards competition between religions, with the sense that an individual could choose rather than amalgamate (North 1992). The objections raised against Christianity, to which Cyprian had to respond (**II 29**; and see above, pp. 72–3), and the banishment of Manichaeism, are only understandable if at least some people believed they were a threat. These people, almost by definition, adhered to traditional religion – and sometimes wanted old traditions to resurface where they had disappeared (**II 46**; and see above, p. 68). The creation of pagan army priests in the third century – probably during the reign of Elagabalus – shows how traditional religion still flourished, but also how it was sufficiently affected by change to allow for the creation of such an institution (Haensch 2006). The *Feriale Duranum* (**II 26**) emphasises continuity in public worship as much as do the above-mentioned percentages of inscriptions to traditional deities. The first sacrifices mentioned in the calendar are the ones to the Capitoline triad of Jupiter, Juno and Minerva. Other gods whose worship is mentioned are Mars and Vesta. The festivals which are referred to are the ancient Quinquatria (a ceremony to purify armour), the birthday of Rome, the festival for Neptune and the Rose festival, at which standards were adorned with roses. If it were not for the first lines which date the document and the names of late second-century *divi*, the calendar could have been issued much earlier than the reign of the last Severan emperor. Similarly, in AD 198/9 a document was distributed in the reign of the first ruler of that dynasty (**II 34**). Although the ban on magical consultation was issued by the Egyptian prefect, Quintus Aemilius Saturninus, the emperor himself was doubtless involved. He would not have objected so much if he did not believe in the effectiveness of such consultation. One could interpret this as yet another instance of an increasingly dictatorial imperial behaviour in all aspects of life, or fear of opposition in increasingly fraught times. Long before, however, in supposedly happy times, Vespasian had banished all astrologers from Rome (Dio Cassius 66.9.2). In tetrarchic times, Diocletian minted coins proclaiming the 'Genius of the Roman people' (see above, p. 52) and defended imperial power by emphasising links with Jupiter and Hercules: 'hardly a sign of paganism shrinking' (MacMullen 1981: 127). In the third century, there was religious change, of course, but continuity too.

Conclusion

Fragmentation and unification from 193 to 284

On 20 November 284, Diocles, the former commander of Numerian's imperial guard, was declared emperor. Though there were indications to the contrary, Diocles declared that he was not to blame for the murder of his predecessor. The real criminal had been the praetorian prefect Lucius Aper, Diocles claimed:

> Then, assuming the tone of a sovereign and a judge, he commanded that Aper should be brought in chains to the foot of the tribunal. 'This man', said he, 'is the murderer of Numerian'; and without giving him time to enter on a dangerous justification, drew his sword, and buried it in the breast of the unfortunate praefect. A charge supported by such decisive proof was admitted without contradiction, and the legions, with repeated acclamations, acknowledged the justice and authority of the emperor Diocletian. (Gibbon 1776: I, ch. 12)

An individual who had lived through the previous half century might have been unsurprised about the way this new emperor came to power. It had been done before. Through far-reaching reforms, Diocletian did his utmost to prevent this way of obtaining imperial power from being used again. The fact that he abdicated of his own accord and died of ill health rather than assassination shows some of his success. Diocletian's organisational measures doubtlessly helped the empire overcome trouble, but it is a measure of the success of third-century Roman actions that on his accession to the throne the empire was still standing, geographically hardly smaller than at the death of Commodus on 31 December AD 192.

The 91 years between Commodus' and Numerian's deaths had doubtless shaken the Roman world. Throughout the period, the empire had seen fragmentation. Never before had there been so many emperors and usurpers in so little time, and never before had large sections of the empire actually seceded (see above, Chapter 1). Nor was there only political fragmentation: the rise of Christianity and Manichaeism showed how 'outsiders' were becoming increasingly prominent (see above, Chapter 5). At the same time, these 91 years had seen unification: emperorship became ever more important, even if emperors lost power (see above, Chapter 4). A general sense of Roman-ness increased, even where the importance of Rome diminished. Collective citizenship was essential in this, of course, and made Roman law universal (see above, Chapter 3). It may even have been a first step towards a unified Roman religion. In such an interpretation, Christianity and 'religious fragmentation' only came to the fore after multiple religions in the Roman Empire were replaced by notions of one Roman religion. Fragmentation may in this case have been an (unwanted) result of unification. Similarly, secession by Postumus and Zenobia may well have kept the Gallic and Palmyrene Empires safe from further harm, giving Aurelian the possibility of reincorporating them in the Roman Empire. Temporary fragmentation allowed for later reunification. Fragmentation and unification need not always function in opposition. There had, in any case, always been an implicit fragmentation in the empire, with different regions having different climates and economic developments. The many external threats and consequent warfare which characterised third-century history deepened this differentiation. Some areas suffered much more than others in economic and military terms. Especially in those areas which suffered more, the importance of the military became most pronounced (see above, Chapter 2). At the end of the third century local differences had become much more pronounced. But in this local reality individuals may have become more 'Roman' than ever before. The altar that Masius and Titianus Ianuari dedicated to 'the safety of the empire' (**II 16 13.7844**) shows how the empire's welfare had become a concept which people could relate to. Ironically, the notion of real Roman unity arose in an era of fragmentation.

A third-century crisis?

An offering for the safety of the whole Roman Empire also shows that some people perceived the empire as a whole to be at risk. To use perhaps the most discussed term concerning third-century history, Masius and Titianus Ianuari may have believed the empire to have been in crisis. The notion of a 'third-century crisis', however, is a laden one. There is not so much discussion of whether there were crises in the third century – that seems to be obvious to all – as of whether the era as a whole should be described as a crisis. The first attempts to describe such an age of crisis were made by the French scholar Léon Homo, in 1913, followed by the great Russian scholar Michael Rostovtzeff in 1923 (Homo 1913; Rostovtzeff 1923). The first edition of the volume of the *CAH* dealing with the period 193–224 followed suit and was called *The Imperial Crisis and Recovery* (1939). In the 1970s the notion was strengthened by important publications by MacMullen and Alföldy, who emphasised continuous instability, increasing influence of the military and military provinces, economic problems and religious decline. All attention went to keeping the empire intact against foreign invasions, at the cost of all earlier conventions (MacMullen 1976: 195–213; Alföldy 1974).

Lately, however, counter-arguments have been brought forward, especially in the German-speaking world (Strobel 1993; Witschel 1999). Rather than speaking of crisis, which is deemed judgemental, one should talk of 'change' and 'transformation'. More importantly, detailed regional analysis of archaeological remains shows that socio-economic change was very different from one province to the next, and that in many zones of the empire, inhabitants seem to have been doing well for much of the third century. Even where there were troubles, they had been foreshadowed in earlier ages (see above, Chapter 2). Finally, many of the essential parts of Roman-ness, not least among which are the literary culture, the basic organisational structure of the economy, and indeed the empire itself, survived the third-century problems and are continuously recognisable in the Roman Empire of the fourth century. These points have also affected thinking in the Anglo-Saxon world, though not, perhaps, the titles of works on the period, which still mention crisis or use a semi-synonym and state that the empire was 'at bay' (Potter 2004).

There have, in turn, been scholars defending the notion of crisis. They argue that the loss of position of the city of Rome and her Senate, combined with a change in local elite behaviour and in the position of traditional religion, show a profound change of mentality (Liebe-schuetz 2007: 17–18). Also, it has been argued that the likes of Masius and Titianus Ianuari felt the empire to be under threat, showing a 'crisis mentality' (Eck 2007: 32–4).

A decisive stance is impossible, but some points should be clear by now. Politically and militarily, there were real problems in the Roman Empire, certainly from the death of Gordian III onwards. Even if not all areas were affected in the same way, the secession of sections of the empire will have been known and discussed throughout the empire.

More clearly still, the rapid turnover of emperors, all making efforts to be as visible as possible, was also noticeable in areas of relative peace. The many petitions to the different emperors illustrate how well people in the province were aware of who ruled them (see above, Chapter 1 and 4). The same holds for Roman provincial coins, which, until their disappearance, continuously depict the ruling emperor on the obverse. People were willing to defend the empire, and did so effectively, but they cannot have failed to notice that the Roman world was less than before defended by actions which originated directly from the centre. There are simply no first- or second-century examples of emperors dying on the battleground, or being captured by the enemy (see above, Chapter 1).

From the 240s, then, one could speak of a military and political crisis, but in socio-economic terms there is less clarity. In this respect, the local differences are pronounced, and as long as there was no fighting and soldiers were not stationed too near, zones could still thrive. The increased importance of military men and procurators of imperial estates may have been pronounced, but it did not affect everyone in the same way. Nor did it stop members of the traditional elites from occupying important (non-military) positions in Rome and Italy. Soldiers had been problematic in earlier times as well (**II 19**) though in the third century emperors seem to have reacted less stringently (**II 16 3.12336**). In terms of legal developments, and of citizenship, the third century started with what may well be described as the high tide of Roman imperial history. Papyri show how the *Constitutio Antoniniana* continuously affected inhabitants of the empire, even in the 260s, when militarily matters were going very wrong (see above, Chapter 3; **II 23 12.1467**). Continuously, also, people looked to the emperors to lead them. Political realities bore seemingly no relation to the development of emperorship – apart from raising emperorship away from reality towards the divine. This was an important development and was at least partially a reaction to the disappearance of normal modes of legitimation (see above, Chapter 4). Another, probably partial, reaction was the persecution of Christianity. Problems were blamed on a group of people who disregarded traditional religion. Still, it is unlikely that the rise of Christianity itself was the result of military problems. At the same time, their rise in prominence made Christians more of a threat than they had been in earlier times. Paganism was still a dominant force, and it would need the long reign of Constantine (306–37) and his highly debated conversion to change the balance. In the third century, traditional religion was hardly in decline (see above, Chapter 5).

Inevitably, in a book of this size, much that is relevant for third-century history has remained unsaid. Nor should any period really be looked at in isolation. The Roman Empire had always been transforming. Indeed, its ability to adapt in the face of internal and external threats to a large extent explains its longevity. External threats were more pronounced in the period from AD 193 to AD 284 and adaptations had to be more rapid. But there were almost always traces of continuity. The third century may be characterised by the fact that it had to react continuously to discontinuities. There were certainly third-century crises, possibly even an empire-wide crisis in the years after 260, when financial problems became ever more pronounced. But whatever term is used to describe the period, it should not make historians forget to look at what sources tell us about the inhabitants of the empire. In Rome and its provinces, life went on – crisis or not.

Part II

Documents

1. Cassius Dio: *Roman History* (c. 220)
Translated from the Greek

[74.11.2] Didius Julianus was an insatiable money-maker and extravagant spender, and always desirous of revolution, which is why Commodus had had him exiled to Mediolanum [Milan], Commodus' native city. So as soon as he heard of the death of Pertinax, he hurried to the camp, and standing in front of the gates he began to beseech the soldiers for sovereignty over the Romans.

Whereupon a most disgraceful business, unworthy of Rome, took place. Just as in the market-place or in some auction-room Rome herself and her whole empire were sold at auction. Those who had killed their own emperor were doing the selling, and the buyers, Sulpicianus and Julianus, were competing with each other, one from inside, and one outside. And little by little they advanced, offering as much as 5,000 drachmas per man. Some of the soldiers would bring a message to Julianus, saying 'this is how much Sulpicianus is giving; so what do you offer?' And then to Sulpicianus 'Julianus promises this much; so what do you promise?' And Sulpicianus would have prevailed, since he was on the inside and was prefect of the city, and was the first to quote 5,000 drachmas; but Julianus, rather than any small amount, outbid him by 1,250 drachmas all at once, shouting it out loudly and also signalling with his hands. The soldiers were enraptured by his excess and were at the same time afraid that Sulpicianus might avenge Pertinax, as Julianus kept suggesting to them, so they received him and appointed him emperor.

[74.14.3] These are the things that happened in Rome, and now I will speak of what happened outside it and the rebellions that were attempted. For during that time there were three men, each of whom was in command of three legions of citizens and many foreigners, who laid claim to power. These were Severus, governor of Pannonia, Niger, governor of Syria, and Albinus, governor of Britain. It was these men, then, that were foretold by the three stars which suddenly appeared and surrounded the sun, when Julianus was performing the appropriate sacrifices at the beginning of his reign in front of the Senate house while we were all there. They were so very obvious that even the soldiers kept looking up at them and pointing them out to each other; furthermore,

89

they were spreading the opinion that something terrible would come upon Julianus. But although we most of all hoped and prayed that this would happen, we did not dare to look up at the stars, on account of the fear that gripped us, except for sideways glances. This much I myself experienced.

[74.16.1] After Julianus learned of these things he had Severus made an enemy by the senate, and began to prepare for him; he fortified the area around the city with a ditch and placed gates inside it so that he could take the field there and fight from it. [2] And the whole city was at that time nothing but an army camp, as though in enemy country. There was great confusion among each of the troops (men, horses and elephants) who were bivouacking and training, and everyone else was very much afraid of the armed men, since the soldiers hated them. [3] But it is also the case that laughter used to overcome us, because the praetorians did nothing to live up to their name or their promises: they had learnt to live genteelly. The marines were sent for from the fleet that lay in harbour in Misenum, but they did not even know how to drill, and the elephants, weighed down by the howdahs on their backs, refused to carry their riders and threw them off. [4] We laughed particularly when Julianus strengthened the palace with latticed gates and strong doors, because he believed that, since the soldiers probably would not have killed Pertinax so easily if he had been shut up, he could lock himself in if he was defeated and survive. [5] He slew Laetus and Marcia, so all those who had plotted against Commodus were destroyed (for later Severus threw Narcissus to the beasts, having it announced that 'this is the man who strangled Commodus'), and he killed many children for magical purposes, in order to find out what was to come in the future and be able to deflect it. And he kept sending people after Severus to murder him treacherously.

[77.10.1] At this time an Italian named Bulla, having organised a band of robbers numbering 600 men, ravaged Italy for two years, despite the presence of the emperors and many soldiers. [2] And although he was hunted by many men, Severus casting after him eagerly, whenever Bulla was seen he was nowhere to be seen, whenever found he was nowhere to be found, when caught he was never captured; for he made use of both great munificence and great cunning. He learnt of everyone who was coming out of Rome and all those putting in at Brundisium [Brindisi], how many they were and what they had in their possession. [3] He took a part of the belongings of most of those he waylaid and let them go straightaway. Those who were craftsmen he held back for some time, and after he had made use of their skills he paid them a fee and let them go. When two of his brigands were captured and were about to be thrown to the animals, he went up to the gaoler pretending that he was a magistrate of the city and that he wanted some men of their particular type. So in this way he took possession of them and rescued them. [4] He also went up to the centurion who was in charge of stamping out brigandry and, pretending to be someone else, denounced himself, and promised that if the centurion followed him he would hand over the robber chief to him. And, pretending to lead the centurion to Felix (for this was another of his names), he took him to a hollow place surrounded by overgrown bushes and easily captured him. [5] Whereupon he dressed himself as a magistrate and stood on the tribunal. He then summoned the centurion, shaved his head, and said 'tell your masters that they must look after their slaves, or they will become robbers'. For he had many imperial freedmen in his gang, some of whom had been badly paid, some not paid at all. [6] As Severus learnt of each of these actions he said angrily 'I am winning battles in Britain by means of others; in Italy I myself have become weaker than a brigand'. At last he despatched a military tribune from his bodyguards with many horsemen, threatening him with terrible punishments if he did not bring back Bulla in chains. This man learnt that Bulla was sleeping with another man's wife and he persuaded her to help them, on the promise of an amnesty for her husband. [7] Consequently Bulla was taken, asleep in a cave. Papinianus the prefect asked him 'why were you a robber?' and he answered 'why are *you* a prefect?' After this public notice was given of his death by wild beasts, and his gang also fell apart; it seems in him alone was the whole strength of the six hundred.

[77.15.2] After this had happened the Caledonians took part in the rebellion of the Maeatae, and Severus prepared to wage war on them himself. But a sickness took hold of him on the fourth of February, while he was in the process of doing so, with, so they say, Antoninus helping it along. At any rate, before he died he is reported to have said the following to his sons (I will pass on only his actual words, not embellishing them): 'be harmonious, enrich the soldiers, scorn everything else'. After this his body was dressed in military uniform and placed on a pyre. The soldiers and his sons honoured him by marching round the pyre, and the gifts which the soldiers present had brought were thrown on before his sons lit the fire. Afterwards the bones were put into an urn of purple stone, carried back to Rome and placed in the imperial mausoleum. And it is said that just before he died Severus sent for the urn, felt it and announced 'you will hold a man whom the whole world could not contain'.

[77.16.4] Again, he [Septimius Severus] reprimanded people who were not chaste, and even formulated certain laws against adultery. As a result there was a tremendous number of accusations for that offence (when I was consul, for instance, I found that 3,000 cases were put forwards) but, since only very few people prosecuted these offences, he also stopped dealing with them.

[78.9.1] Antoninus was deeply impressed by Alexander; he used one pretext after another, war after war, to excuse his fondness for spending money on the soldiers, very many of whom he kept by him. He made it his business to rob, defraud and bankrupt every other man, not least the senators. [2] There were the gold crowns which he constantly used to demand, as though he were always winning battles (by this I do not mean the construction of the crowns themselves, for what does that cost? But the cities were in the habit of giving large amounts of money for the sake of this 'crowning' of the emperor). [3] There were the many provisions from all quarters, gifts which we lavished on him and paid for. All of these he gave straight to the soldiers or sold. [4] Then there were the presents he demanded from rich private citizens and the commons, and the new duties and other taxes he imposed. These were in addition to the tithe he imposed instead of the five percent tax on emancipated slaves and on bequests that people inherited, and all gifts. [5] The rights of inheritance and tax exemptions which applied to those who were closely related to the deceased he brought to an end (this was the reason why he admitted everyone in the empire to Roman citizenship; he claimed it was an honour, but in fact it was so that he could make something out of it: foreigners did not have to contribute to most of these taxes). [6] Apart from all of these impositions there were also the houses of every kind whenever he rushed out of Rome, the very expensive quarters at which to break his journeys, and the accommodation expenses for even the briefest, all of which we were forced to furnish. He never stayed in them, nor ever intended even to see them. [7] Furthermore, we provided wild beast shows and horse races everywhere, wherever he wintered or even thought he might winter. They were all destroyed straightaway. There was only one reason for this to happen: to ruin us.

[78.16.4] This is also what he [Caracalla] did to anyone who committed adultery. Although he engaged in more adultery than anyone else, as much as he possibly could, he hated the others who shared this vice and killed them, against all precedent. And he was aggrieved by men of good character, but gave the impression of appreciating some of them once they were dead.

[79.36. 1] Macrinus also wrote to the senate about this false Antoninus the same things which he wrote to all the governors, calling him a young boy and saying that he was unstable. He also wrote to Maximus the prefect of the city, discussing the appropriate matters and saying that even the soldiers who had just enlisted were demanding everything that the longer-serving soldiers had: those who had not been granted the money and those who had been deprived of nothing were equally angry. [2] Even if one left to one side all the things which Severus and his sons had found to destroy the professionalism of the army, he stated that it would be impossible to give them their full pay as well as the donatives which they already had [3] (for Tarautus had extended the increase in their wages to 17,000 drachmas a year), and impossible not to give it, for this … and that … lawful … but these … expenses … this, then, … [4] and the public … military … and … ruin … it was possible … the boy as … and upon himself … himself … and that he regretted that he even had a son. He said he had a consolation in his misfortune, which was that he had survived that brother-killer, who had endeavoured to destroy the world. [5] And then he even added this 'I know there are many who would eagerly prefer to murder an emperor than survive themselves. But I can say this about myself, that there is no one who would hope or pray that I were destroyed.' Whereupon Fulvius Giogenianus shouted out 'we have all prayed for that'.

[80.4.1] So although he was a man of this sort and had a name appropriate to mimes and buffoonery, Comazo was commander of the praetorian guard, never having been tested out in even a single position of trust or leadership, except for his stint in the army. [2] He also received consular honours, and afterwards even became consul and prefect of the city, not only once, but twice and indeed three times, which had never been never permitted to another man before. This too, then, can be numbered among the most unlawful doings of Avitus. [3] So Attalus died because of Comazo, and Triccianus on account of the Albans, whom he had led in a disciplined way under Macrinus; Castinus because he was efficient and known to many of the soldiers due to the generalships he had held, and because he was acquainted with Antoninus. [4] Consequently he had been spending his time in Bithynia, where Macrinus had sent him for other reasons. But Avitus killed him, but nonetheless he wrote to the Senate that he was reinstating Castinus after his exile by Macrinus, as also Julius Asper. [5] Sulla died too, who had governed Cappadocia, although he had been removed from it, because he meddled in something, and because when Avitus banished him from Rome he met with the Gaulish soldiers coming home after wintering in Bithynia, where they had stirred up trouble. [6] For such reasons these men were destroyed, and no message about their fate was sent to the senate. And Seius Carus, the grandson of Fuscian the prefect of the city, died because he was rich and important and intelligent; the pretext was that he too had associated with some soldiers encamped on the Alban Mount (he heard the evidence against him in the palace, Avitus alone prosecuting, and he died there too). [7] Valerius Paetus was killed because he modelled some gold-plated images of himself as decorations for his mistress; these were the grounds for the accusation that he was going to go to Cappadocia, next to his home province (he was Galatian), intent on revolution, and this was why he was making gold pieces featuring his own engraved image.

2. Herodian: *History of the Empire after Marcus* (c. 240)
Translated from the Greek

[3.8.4-5] Severus went to the sanctuary of Jupiter, carried out the remaining rites and headed back to the palace, whereupon he distributed large handouts to the people, to celebrate his victories. But he gave the most to the soldiers, and conceded many other things that had not previously been allowed. He first increased their provision-money, then permitted them to wear gold rings and to cohabit with their wives. These were all measures which were usually considered to be deleterious to military self-control, war-readiness and preparation. And he was the first to overturn altogether their robust and austere mode of life, obedience in carrying out their duties, and discipline and modesty towards their generals: he taught them to hunt after money and diverted them towards luxury.

[4.2] It is Roman custom to deify the emperors when they die and their children succeed them: they call this honour apotheosis. Grieving can be seen throughout the city, along with feasting and worship. For they bury the body of the dead man in a lavish funeral, as humans do; they make a wax image identical to the dead man and put it on top of a huge ivory bier, on which is spread bedding made of gold cloth. This they set up at the entrance to the palace. This image lies there looking like someone pale and ill, and the mourners sit around the bier for most of the day. All the senators sit on the left-hand side, wearing black cloaks, and on the right sit all the women whose husbands or fathers are of a high enough rank for such an honour. None of them sports any gold ornaments or is decked out with gold necklaces. They wear blank white clothes and look like mourners. For seven days these rituals are carried out ; and periodically doctors will approach the bier and go up to it, giving it an actual examination, and each time announcing that the invalid's condition is more serious. When he appears to have died, the most well-born of the order of knights and chosen young men of the senate lift up the bier and carry it along the Sacred Way.

They take it to the old forum, where Roman consuls resign their year in office. On either side platforms are set up like seats in a theatre; on one side a chorus of the noblest and most well-born children stands, on the opposite side of women who have the best reputation. They each sing hymns and paeans to the dead man, which are perfectly rendered in a solemn and dirge-like measure. After this they lift up the bier and carry it outside the city to a plain called the Campus Martius, where a square and even-sided construction is built in the flattest part of the plain. It consists only of wood, great planks forming a framework that looks like a house, and it is filled inside with firewood. The outside is decorated with sheets of gold-embroidered cloth and ivory ornaments, along with beautiful pictures. On top of this another smaller building is placed, the same shape and similarly decorated, with open gates and doors. A third and a fourth are added, each one smaller than the one below it, until the smallest one is put on. You could compare the layout of the building to the beacon-towers which are placed in harbours and at night lead ships into safe landing-points with their fire; most people call these Pharoi.

They carry the bier up and place it in the second of these buildings, scattering and pouring out spices and incense of every type which the earth supplies, and every fruit and herb on the planet which is gathered for its pleasant smell. There is no tribe or city, or person of rank or honour, who does not compete for glory by sending these last gifts to honour the emperor. And when this great mound of spices has been piled up and the whole place is full, an exercise on horseback is performed around the building, and the entire order of knights forms up in a wheeling formation and rides round in a circle, following a pyrrhic course and rhythm. A similar formation of chariots goes around, carrying riders wearing purple-edged robes, and wearing masks with the likenesses of Romans who have led armies or governed successfully.

When all this is done the man who is to take on the empire picks up a torch and lights the building, and the rest kindle the fire from every side. The fire easily and swiftly catches the whole thing, the quantities of firewood and incense being set alight. And from the last and smallest building , as though from a battlement, an eagle is let loose, escaping with the fire into the sky; it is believed by the Romans to carry the soul of the emperor from the earth to heaven, and afterwards he is worshipped along with the rest of the gods.

[4.4] The hatred and discord kept increasing. Whenever generals or governors had to be appointed, each one sought to favour his own friends, and if they were judging a case, they always took opposing views – this sometimes had fatal results for those whose cases they were in charge of. They were far keener to argue than to provide justice. They even supported different teams at shows. They were always preparing every kind of plot, bribing wine-waiters and cooks to use fatal poisons. Neither had great success, since each led his life carefully and constantly on his guard. Finally, Antoninus [Caracalla], driven by his desire to rule alone, could bear it no longer. He resolved to strike out or fall with dignity, to resort to cold steel and murder. Since his furtive plotting had not met with success, he was driven by necessity to dangerous and desperate measures.

...

Geta, mortally wounded, gushed blood on his mother's breast, and relinquished his hold on life. And Antoninus, the murder accomplished, sprang at a run out of the chamber and rushed through the whole palace, yelling about the great danger he had escaped, and how he had barely survived. He ordered the soldiers who were on guard at the palace to surround him and take him off to the camp, saying that he might be safe if guarded there, while he would be killed if he stayed in the palace. They believed him, not knowing what had happened inside, and they all set off, carrying him along at a run. This caused disorder as the people saw the emperor being hurried through the middle of the city during the evening. So Antoninus rushed into the camp and into the sanctuary there, prostrating himself before the camp standards and images. He threw himself to the ground and pledged thank-offerings and made sacrifices in gratitude for his deliverance. As the news went around the soldiers, some of whom were having baths, and others of whom were asleep, they all ran together, stricken by panic. Antoninus appeared, but did not say exactly what had happened; rather he shouted that he had evaded the perilous scheming of an enemy of himself and of the state (which is to say his brother), and that he had scarcely prevailed, after a great struggle, over this enemy; both of them had been in danger, and fate had protected one emperor. Expressing himself in this oblique sort of way, he wanted what he had done to be understood rather than actually heard. And he promised them 2,500 Attic drachmas per soldier, and he added half again of what they were already paid in the provision-money. He told them to go and take the money from the temples and treasuries, lavishly bedewing on them in one day everything which Severus had taken eighteen years to gather and store away after he had taken it from others. This great amount of money caught the soldiers' attention, and now understanding the situation (because those who had fled from inside the palace were telling of the murder), they publicly proclaimed Antoninus emperor and announced that Geta was an enemy of the state.

[7.3. 5] After Maximinus had ruined most of the distinguished men and seized their land, he began to consider this to be small and insignificant and not enough for his purposes, and he turned to the public treasuries. He took for his personal profit all money which had been collected for the common people's benefit or for gifts, and all the funds which were kept for games or religious festivals. He handed over to the mints the dedications to the temples, the statues of the gods, the honours of *divi*, and decorations on public buildings or the city adornments, in short, any material suitable to make into coins.

3. *Historia Augusta* (late fourth century)
Translated from the Latin

a. *Life of Gallienus*
[2.6] In Illyricum, having with him one of his sons and commanding 30,000 soldiers, he engaged in battle with a general of the emperor Aureolus, with the name of Domitian, who had assumed power against Gallienus.

[13.1–5] At the same time, Odaenathus was treacherously slain by his cousin, and with him his son Herodes, whom he himself had called imperator. Then Zenobia, his wife, herself took power, because his remaining sons, Herennianus and Timolaus, were too young. She ruled for a long time, neither womanlike nor in a feminine way, but with more courage and intelligence not just than Gallienus – any girl could have ruled better than him – but even than many other emperors. As to Gallienus, when he heard that Odaenathus was killed, he prepared for war with the Persians as a late vindication of his father, and acted like an intelligent *princeps* after his general Heraclianus had gathered soldiers. However, this Heraclianus, when he was set against the Persians, was defeated by the Palmyrenes and lost all the soldiers which he had gathered, since Zenobia was ruling Palmyra and the East with the strength of a man.

[13.6-8] At the same time the Scythians crossed the Euxine [Black] Sea, entered Histrum, and committed many atrocities on Roman soil. When he found out about these Gallienus put the Byzantines Cleodamus and Athenaeus in charge of restoring and fortifying the cities. There was a battle near Pontus, and the barbarians were defeated by the Byzantine generals. The Goths were then defeated in a naval battle at sea, with Venerianus acting as admiral, but Venerianus hiself died during the fighting. Then they devastated Cyzicum and Asia, and finally all of Greece, but they were defeated by the Athenians, who were led by Dexippus, a historian of the time. Ejected from that area they wandered through Epirum, Macedonia and Boeotia.

b. *Life of Tacitus*
[9.5] He ordered that a temple be built to the deified emperors, in which should be the statues of the good *principes*, so that libations might be given to them on their birthdays, on the Parilia, and on the Kalends of January for the Vows.

4. Sextus Aurelius Victor: *Book of the Caesars* (c. 361)
Translated from the Latin

[26] After these two had possessed the highest power for two years, and had prosecuted a war against the Germans with some success, all of a sudden the army made Antonius Gordianus, proconsul of Africa, emperor at the town of Thydrum, although he was not there. This alone could not make him emperor: when he was summoned back, he reached Thydrum to find a mutiny in progress. However, he easily calmed it and made for Carthage. There, in the hope of averting bad

omens, the fear of which made him quite reasonably anxious, he performed the customary auguries, whereupon one of the victims promptly gave birth. The soothsayers, and indeed he himself (for he was excessively knowledgeable in the use of this science) took this to mean that he was destined to die, but that he would produce the empire for his children. They went on further with their prophecy, also announcing the death of his son, saying that he would be as gentle and harmless as the victim, but that he would not last long, and would be surrounded by conspiracies. Meanwhile it was reported at Rome that Gordianus had actually died, and at the urging of Domitius the praetorian cohorts openly slew the prefect of the city and the other magistrates. In fact Gordianus, after he realised that he had attained the imperial power, had held out the promise of generous rewards and sent legates and letters to Rome. Since he was dead the soldiers had become frustrated and angst ridden, they being the type rather greedy for money, and only ever in search of promises and gifts. But the Senate were afraid that without anyone in charge even more horrible things might befall the city, which already looked as though it had been captured. First they took turns, then they entrusted power to their juniors, making Clodius Pupienus and Caecilius Balbinus Caesars.

[27] While they made their way through Africa the soldiers appointed Gordianus and his son Augusti. The boy, though under age, had been accompanying his father, and was subsequently made praetorian prefect. The nobles did not in fact object to this deed. At last he was summoned to Rome, where the bands of praetorians were destroyed in battle from the top to the very bottom of the city by fighting-parties of gladiators and an army of raw recruits. While all this was occurring at Rome the two Julii Maximini, who were be in Thrace at the time, heard of what was happening and immediately set out for Italy. Pupienus Aquileia laid siege to them and defeated them in battle, whereupon the remainder of their army little by little deserted, and they were killed. With delays of this sort their reign was extended into a third year. With little military uproar Clodius and Caecilius were killed at Rome inside the palace and Gordianus became sole emperor. In that year he renewed and expanded the lustral games, which Nero had introduced to Rome, and set out for Persia, first opening the gates of the temple of Janus, which Marcus had closed, in the traditional manner. There he waged war successfully, but perished in his sixth year in power as the result of a conspiracy by Marcus Philippus the Praetorian Prefect.

[32] But the soldiers, who had been gathered from all sides because of the war that was threatening, and were waiting around in Raetia, conferred power on Licinius Valerianus. Although he was of noble enough family, he was engaged in military service, as was the habit at that time. The Senate made his son Gallienus Caesar, and although it was high summer the Tiber promptly overflowed, as though in spate. Wise men prophesied danger to the state from the young man's fickle nature, because he had been in Etruria when he was summoned, where the ominous flood also came from. And indeed this is what immediately happened: his father was waging a lengthy and indeterminate war in Mesopotamia when he was captured by the foul trickery of the Persian king, who was called Sapor. He was torn to pieces and died in his sixth year as emperor, in fairly hale old age.

[33] At the same moment plague devastated Rome, which happens often in periods of intolerable fears, when minds despair. [Gallienus] himself, when this was going on, visited bars and eating places, retained friendship with pimps and drunks, and gave too much attention to his wife Salonina and to an embarrassing affair with the daughter of a king of the Germans, Attalus, whose name was Pipa. For this reason, far more dreadful civil wars erupted. Because first of all Postumus, who turned out to be in charge of the barbarians in Gaul, took imperial power. After he had chased away a tribe of Germans, he fought a war with Laelian. Him he defeated just as easily, but he then fell through rebellion of his own men. Apparently, notwithstanding their insistence, he had refused to allow them to plunder the inhabitants of Mainz for supporting Laelian …

… In fact senators were annoyed [by Gallienus] about abusing their ranks, because on top of the general evil of the Roman world, he was the first to forbid senators to engage in a military career or enter into the army, because he was afraid that the imperial power would be transferred to the best of the *nobiles* because of his own indolence. He was in power for nine years.

[36] Finally, then, about half a year after Aurelian's death, the Senate made Tacitus emperor, one of the ex-consuls. He was indeed a gentle man, and almost all were happier since senators had regained from the arrogant soldiers the right to elect the emperor. But this happiness was short, nor was the end tolerable. Because Tacitus died as soon as the two hundreth day of his reign at Tyana. But earlier he had tortured to death those responsible for the death of Aurelian, and especially their leader

Mucapor, who had actually killed him. And his [Tacitus'] brother Florianus took power, without any advice of the senate or the military.

[37] ... From this moment onwards, the power of the soldiers increased, and the right of the Senate to create emperors disappeared for as long as we can remember. It is uncertain whether the Senate wanted this for indifference and fear, or for hatred of conflicts. It could have regained the right to military careers, which had been forbidden in the edict that Gallienus had issued, during the reign of Tacitus, when the legions were amenable. Florianus would not have dared take power through the decision of ordinary soldiers, nor would it have been given to anyone, who thought it right, if that most eminent order had been serving in the forts ...

[39] ... Their native land was actually Illyricum: and although they had little concern with culture, they were sufficiently seasoned in the hardship of countryside and military camp to be the best rulers for the state. Therefore it is clear that men are better made respectable and mindful by suffering hardship. Those who have not suffered hard times and judge everybody by their own experiences are, on the other hand, less thoughtful.

5. Eutropius: *Breviarium* (c. 369)
Translated from the Latin

[8.16] Pertinax succeeded him, now an old man who had reached his seventies. He was then prefect of the city and was ordered to rule by decree of the senate. On the eightieth day of his reign plotting by the praetorian guard and the wickedness of Julianus led to his death.

[8.17] After him Salvius Julianus took up the empire; he was a nobleman and extremely learned in law, the grandson of that Salvius Julianus who had composed the edict promulgated by the Divine Hadrian at the start of his reign. He was defeated by Severus at the Milvian Bridge and was murdered in the palace. He lived for seven months after he began to rule.

[8.18] After him Septimius Severus received the running of the Roman Empire. He came from Africa, from Lepcis in the province of Tripolitania. He was the only emperor in memory both before or afterwards to come from Africa. He was first advocate of the treasury, then military tribune, and he came to the administration of the entire empire by way of many and varied positions and honours. He wanted to be called Pertinax in honour of the Pertinax who had been killed by Julianus. He was quite thrifty, and savage by nature. He succesfully waged many wars. He killed Pescennius Niger, who had raised a rebellion in Egypt and Syria. He conquered the Parthians, the inner Arabs and the Adiabenes and was consequently called Parthicus, Arabicus, Adiabenicus. He restored many things throughout the Roman world. Under him even Clodius Albinus, who had been an accomplice of Julianus in killing Pertinax, and who had made himself Caesar in Gaul, was defeated and slain at Lugdunum.

[8.19] But Severus, in addition to his success in war, was even famous for his civilian enthusiasms: he was learned in literary matters and had fully grasped the knowledge of philosophy. He started campaigning in Britain again and protected the provinces he gained in perfect safety behind a wall which he built for 132 miles, from sea to sea. He died quite an old man at Eboracum, sixteen years and three months into his reign. He was made a god. He also left two sons to be his successors, Bassianus and Geta, though he asked the senate to decree the name of Antoninus upon Bassianus. So he was called Marcus Aurelius Antoninus Bassianus and succeeded his father. Geta had been named an enemy of the state and promptly died.

[8.20] Marcus Aurelius Antoninus Bassianus, then, also known as Caracalla, was almost the same as his father in moral character, but a little harsher and more sinister. He made an outstanding contribution to Rome, in the form of baths which were known as the *thermae Antoninianae*, but did little else memorable. His lust was unrestrained, and he married his step-mother Julia. He died in Osdroena at Edessa, in the process of leading an expedition against Parthia, in the second month of the sixth year of his reign. He was only just forty-four and was given a public burial.

[8.21] Then Opilius Macrinus, who was praetorian prefect, was made emperor along with his son Diadumenus. They had no time for anything memorable: their reign lasted all of a year and two months. They were both killed at the same time in a military rebellion.

[8.22] After them Marcus Aurelius Antoninus was chosen. People thought he was the son of Antoninus Caracalla, but he was actually a priest in the temple of Heliogabalus. Although the soldiers and the senate expected great things when he came to Rome, he defiled himself with every vice. He lived unchastely and obscenely and after two years and eight months he was slain when the soldiers rebelled, his mother Symiasera with him.

[8.23] Aurelius Alexander succeeded him, acclaimed as Caesar by the army, and Augustus by the Senate. He was still a young man, and took up war against the Persians, gloriously defeating Xerxes, their king. He ruthlessly administered military discipline, discharging legions wholesale when they rebelled. He had a judicial assessor or secretary called Ulpian, who codified the law. He was extremely popular at Rome, but died in Gaul when the soldiers rebelled, on the ninth day of his thirteenth year in power. He was uniquely dutiful to his mother Mamaea.

[9.1] After him Maximinus attained power from the ranks of the army, in the first place only by the will of the soldiers; he had no senatorial authority, nor was he a senator himself. He waged war successfully against the Germans, whereupon he was acclaimed emperor by the soldiers, but his troops deserted him, and Pupienus Aquileia killed him along with his son; together they had ruled for three years and a few days.

[9.2] Afterwards there were three Augusti at the same time, Pupienus, Balbinus and Gordianus. The first two were of obscure family, while Gordianus was a nobleman; indeed, his father, the elder Gordianus, had been chosen during the reign of Maximinus as emperor by the soldiers while he held proconsular authority in Africa. But when they came to Rome Balbinus and Pupienus were murdered in the palace, leaving the empire to Gordianus alone. Gordianus was still a boy when he married Tranquillina at Rome, opened the gates of Janus Geminus and set out to the East to wage war on Parthia, which was threatening disruptions. He succeeded and humiliated the Persians in huge battles. On his way back he was killed not far from the bounds of the empire by Philip, who plotted against him and ruled after him. The soldiers raised a tomb for him 20,000 yards from Circesium, which is now a Roman camp looking out over the Euphrates, carried his remains back to Rome and acclaimed him a god.

[9.3] The two Philippi, father and son, took up power after Gordianus had been killed, and brought the army back safely to Italy from Syria. While they were in charge the thousandth year of the city of Rome was celebrated with great magnificence, games and spectacles. The army then murdered them both, Philip the elder at Verona, the younger at Rome. They ruled for five years; however, they were made divine.

[9.4] After them Decius, who was born in Budalia, came to power from Lower Pannonia. He put down a civil war which had begun in Gaul, made his son Caesar and built a bath complex at Rome. When he and his son had reigned for two years they were both murdered in Barbaricum. The father was deservedly enrolled among the gods.

[9.5] Soon Gallus Hostilianus and his son Volusianus were made emperors. Under their rule Aemilianus stirred up revolution in Moesia; they were on their way to putting this down when they were killed, dying at Interamna without managing to reach two years in power. They did nothing particularly impressive: their reign was notable only for plague, sickness and famine.

[9.6] Aemilianus was born entirely unknown, ruled anonymously, and was dead after three months.

[9.7] Licinius Valerianus, governor of Raetia and Noricum, followed him, the army making him emperor and shortly afterwards Augustus. Gallienus too was named Caesar by the Senate in Rome. Their rule was pernicious to the reputation of Rome, and was almost fatal, either because the emperors were unlucky or because they were incompetent. The Germans reached Ravenna. Valerianus, waging war in Mesopotamia, was defeated by Sapor, the Persian king, and was shortly afterwards even taken prisoner, growing old in Parthia in ignoble servitude.

[9.8] Gallienus was made Augustus while still a teenager, first ruling successfully, then adequately, and eventually disastrously. As an energetic young man he achieved much in Gaul and Illyricum, killing Ingenuus, who had assumed the purple, at Mursa, and … Trebellianus. For a long time he was calm and restrained, but eventually he fell into every vice, losing his hold on the state through unforgivable apathy and despair. The Alamanni laid waste to Gaul and penetrated Italy. Dacia, which Trajan had extended past the Danube, was lost, and Greece, Macedonia, Pontus and Asia were despoiled by the Goths. Pannonia was plundered by the Sarmatians and the Quadi; Germans reached as far as Spain and took that noble city Tarraco by storm, while the Parthians occupied Mesopotamia and had begun to take their revenge on Syria.

[9.9] Now things seemed hopeless, and almost the whole Roman Empire had been lost, when Postumus, with no background whatsoever, assumed the purple in Gaul and ruled for ten years with such success that his immense courage and restraint restored the provinces which had been almost entirely consumed. A military rebellion killed him, because he declined to hand over the town of Mogontiacum to the soldiers to pillage. It had risen up against him, Laelianus fomenting the revolt. After him Marius took up imperial power. He was the merest workman, and was killed after two days. Victorinus subsequently came to power in Gaul, an energetic man but too oversexed and given to breaking up other people's marriages, so he was killed at Colonia Agrippinensis by one of his quartermasters, who contrived a plot against him in his second year of power.

[9.10] Tetricus the senator succeeded him, who had the rank of governor, administering Aquitania. The army chose him as emperor in his absence, and he donned the purple at Burdigala, and prevented many other plots by the soldiers. But while these things were happening in Gaul, Odaenathus was conquering the Persians in the East. He defended Syria, won back Mesopotamia and reached as far as Ctesiphon.

[9.11] So when Gallienus abandoned the state, the Roman Empire was preserved by Postumus in the West and Odaenathus in the East. Meanwhile Gallienus was killed in Mediolanum with his brother Valerianus in his ninth year of power, and Claudius succeeded him; he was chosen by the army, and the Senate named him Augustus. He defeated the Goths who were ravaging Illyricum and Macedonia in a great battle. A thrifty man, modest, tenacious in pursuit of justice and fitted to ruling the empire, he nonetheless succumbed to illness before two years were out. He was appointed a god and the Senate honoured him greatly, dedicating a golden shield to him in the Senate house, and a golden statue on the Capitol.

[9.12] Quintillus, brother of Claudius, was named emperor after him with the agreement of the army, a man of unique restraint and humility, the equal of his brother or perhaps superior. The senate agreed to designate him Augustus and he was killed seventeen days into his reign.

[9.13] Aurelianus became emperor after him. He came from Dacia Ripensis and was a powerful warrior, but had an immoderate spirit and was rather prone to cruelty. He too vigorously defeated the Goths. He recalled Roman authority to its former bounds by his success in several wars. He defeated Tetricus in Gaul among the Catalauni; Tetricus betrayed his own troops because he could not bear their constant plotting. In fact, he had even entreated Aurelian in secret messages, using this verse of Virgil among others: 'take me from these evils, unconquered one'. Aurelianus captured Zenobia too, not far from Antioch, without serious warfare. She had ruled the East once her husband Odaenathus had been killed. When he entered Rome he enjoyed a celebrated triumph as saviour of East and West, Tetricus and Zenobia walking before his chariot. As for those two, Tetricus was later governor of Lucania and lived for a very long time as a private citizen; Zenobia left descendants at Rome who still live there.

[9.14] While he ruled even the minters in the city rebelled and debased the coinage, killing a financial officer called Felicissimus. Once he had put down the riot Aurelianus punished them with extreme cruelty. He condemned many noblemen to capital punishment. He was a savage emperor, bloodthirsty, but necessary in some ways, rather than ever lovable. There was. constant slaughter, and he even killed his nephew, but for the most part he put right military discipline and dissolute morals.

[9.15] He built stronger walls around Rome and built a temple to the sun, which he filled with an infinity of gold and jewels. He gave up the province of Dacia, which Trajan had extended past the Danube, because he did not see how he could save it, with all of Illyricum and Moesia devastated. So he removed the Romans from the Dacian cities and fields and gathered them together in the middle of Moesia, calling that Dacia, which now divides two Moesias, and has the Danube flowing into the sea on its right, where previously it was on the left. He was murdered because of a slave's trick: he went to certain soldiers with whom he was friendly, and brought them a list of names which purported to show that Aurelianus was about to kill them; the slave had copied his handwriting. In order to stop him the soldiers killed him in the middle of a journey along the old road between Constantinople and Heraclea; the place is known as Caenophrurium. However, his death did not go unavenged, and he deserved his elevation to the gods.

[9.16] After him Tacitus took power, a man equipped with the best morals and well-suited to ruling the empire. Of course he could provide nothing special when death overtook him within six months. Florianus, who succeeded Tacitus, did nothing in his two months and twenty days in power which is worth remembering.

[9.17] Probus, a man covered in military glory, took hold of the rudder of state after him. He rescued Gaul from the barbarians who were occupying it with a series of immensely successful battles. He bested in battle anyone who tried to seize power, which is to say Saturninus in the East, Proculus and Bonosus at Colonia Agrippinensis. He permitted the Gauls and Pannonians to have vineyards, and used soldiers to set up vineyards on Mount Alma in Sirmium and Aureum in Upper Moesia, and he gave these to provincials to cultivate. After he had waged innumerable wars he said that peace was on the horizon and soon soldiers would no longer be needed. He was a sharp man, vigorous and just, and he was the equal of Aurelianus in military glory, but surpassed him in the peacefulness of his manners. He was still murdered, in an iron-plated tower at Sirmium during a military revolt.

[9.18] Carus was made Augustus after him; he was born in Narbo in

Gaul. He immediately made his sons Carinus and Numerianus Caesars. But while he was waging war against the Sarmatians the news of an uprising by the Persians was announced and he set off East to fight against the Persian nobility. These he routed and took Coches and Ctesiphon, those most noble cities. And while he was in camp above the Tigris he was struck down by a thunderbolt from above. Numerianus his son, whom he had brought with him as Caesar to Persia, was a young man of outstanding natural talent and was having problems with his eyes. Consequently, he was being carried in a litter, where he was killed in a plot instigated by his father-in-law Aper. His death was deceitfully kept hidden until Aper could seize power, but the lie was betrayed by the evil smell of the corpse. For the soldiers who were following him were disturbed by the stench and after some days they pulled away the coverlets in his litter and his death was made known.

[9.19] Meanwhile Carinus, whom Carus, on setting out for Parthia, had left as Caesar in charge of Illyricum, Gaul and Italy, abandoned himself to every kind of wickedness. He killed many innocents on trumped-up charges, ruined noble marriages, and even proved deadly to school-fellows who had twitted him in the lecture room with even the lightest banter. For these reasons everyone hated him and not much later he paid the penalty. For the army, returning in victory from Persia, since it had lost Carus the Augustus to lightning, and Numerianus the Caesar to a conspiracy, made Diocletian emperor. He came from Dalmatia, born in utmost obscurity, so much so that many believe he was the son of a scribe, and some that he was the freedman of the senator Anullinus.

6. Festus: *Breviarium* (c. 370)
Translated from the Latin

[23] It is revolting to recount the fortunes of the unfortunate emperor Valerian. The soldiers had made Valerian emperor, and the senators Gallienus. Valerian, then, joined battle against the Persians in Mesopotamia, and was defeated by Shapur, the king of the Persians. He was captured and withered away in dishonourable servitude. The Persians would have started to make claims on Syria under Gallienus' reign, when they invaded Mesopotamia. But, shameful as it is to recount, the Palmyrenian decurion Odaenathus gave fierce resistance after recruiting a group of Syrian peasants. He dispersed the Persians several times, and so not only managed to defend the border but even made way to Ctesiphon, becoming, astonishingly, the avenger of Roman power.

[24] Zenobia, the wife of Odaenathus, added to the emperor Aurelian's glory, inasmuch as that when her husband died, she held power over the East, through feminine influence. Aurelian, aided by many thousands of armoured cavalry and archers, defeated her at Immae, near Antioch, and led her imprisoned in front of his chariot at his triumph in Rome.

7. Zosimus: *New History* (late fifth century)
Translated from the Greek

[1.39.2] While he was at Emesa celebrating a friend's birthday, he [Odaenathus] lost his life through a conspiracy. Then Zenobia took the power of that region to herself. She was Odaenathus' wife but had the courage of a man and, helped by her husband's friends, acted as well as he had done in all respects.

[1.44.1] Now that the Scythians were scattered, losing a great number of troops, as I have explained, Zenobia began to think about extending her domain …

[1.49.1] When the emperor [Aurelian] heard that the Alamanni and adjoining tribes intended to invade Italy, he was justifiably more concerned for Rome and its vicinity than for the more remote areas of the empire. He therefore ordered sufficient troops to stay defending Pannonia and marched towards Italy. On his route, on the borders of that country near the Ister, he slew many thousands of barbarians in one battle. [2] At the same time, the situation in Rome was problematic. Several senators were sentenced to death after being accused of conspiring against the emperor. Rome, which before had no walls, was surrounded with them. This work started in the reign of Aurelian and was finished by Probus…

[1.50.1] When this was going on in Italy and Pannonia, the emperor prepared to march against the Palmyrenians, who had conquered the whole of Egypt and the East as far as Ancyra in Galatia. They would even have acquired Bithynia as far as Chalcedon if the inhabitants of that area had not shaken off Palmyrene oppression when they heard that Aurelian was made emperor. [2] As soon as the emperor was on his way to march there, Ancyra submitted to the Romans, and then Tuana and all the cities between it and Antioch. He there found Zenobia ready to fight with a large army, as was he, and fought with her as his honour obliged him to do.

[1.54.1] Zenobia was naturally much upset by her defeat, and therefore checked which measures she could take. All were of the opinion that it would be sensible to give up all claims on Emesa, since the Emesenes were set against her and friendly towards the Romans. They advised her to remain within Palmyra, and that when they were secure within that strong city they would discuss the important affairs in tranquility .... [2] ... [Aurelian] then marched immediately to Palmyra, which he surrounded from all sides, whilst his troops were given all kinds of provisions from the neighbouring provinces ...

[1.55.1] ... [The Palmyrenes] then determined to flee across the Euphrates and ask the Persians to create new difficulties for the Romans. [2] Having decided this, they placed Zenobia on a female camel, which is the fastest of that kind of animals and much faster than a horse, and transported her out of the city. Aurelian was very displeased about Zenobia's escape, and according to his tendency for action, he sent out cavalry in pursuit of her. [3] They succeeded in taking her when she was crossing the Euphrates in a boat and brought her to Aurelian. He was pleased at the sight, but with his ambitious character he became uneasy when he thought that in future times it would do no good to his honour to have conquered a woman.

[1.56.2] ... [Aurelian] returned to Emesa, after having made himself master of the city with all the riches it contained, and brought Zenobia and her accomplices to trial. When Zenobia came into court she pleaded strongly in her own defence, putting forward many men who had seduced her, a simple woman ...

8. Publius Aelius Aristides: *To Rome* (143)
Translated from the Greek

[60] What a city is for its frontiers and territories, this city is for the whole world. It is, after all, selected as the general capital for the entire empire. You could say that all those who live in surrounding areas or – constitutionally – in a different country come together around one and the same fortress. She has never rejected anyone and, in fact, takes in all the people of the world, as the ground of the earth carries everybody. She has the following in common with the sea, which, after all does not increase through the rivers' discharge, since fate has decided that she will remain of the same size notwithstanding this increase. Similarly, nothing in the city changes because of its size. As men hide something away in the folds of their clothing, so she accepts and stores away everything, whilst she is and looks the same, despite the arrival and departure of people. [61] We have touched upon this in passing, since it was mentioned. As stated, you, great men, have founded a great city. You

have not made her outstanding by emphasising that nobody could share in this city. No, on the opposite, you have tried to give her a worthy citizenry. 'Roman' you made not just the name of a city but a common people, that is not just one people amongst many, but the one opposing all others. [62] For you do not divide the peoples into Greeks and barbarians, but have divided the peoples into Roman and non-Romans. And you have, in their eyes, not made that division ridiculous, since you – so to speak – have made your city appear to have a higher number of inhabitants than all Greeks combined. To that extent, you have enlarged your city in name. Because of this classification there are at least as many citizens in every town as there are people of their own tribe, even if some of those have never seen the city. There is no need for garrisons on the fortresses. For the greatest and most powerful people of every location guard their own native cities for you. In that way you control the cities doubly: from here, and from each within.

9. The Thirteenth Sibylline Oracle
(mainly written before or in 253)
Translated from the Greek

[1–6] The pure deathless imperishable god who gives power to kings and takes it away, and he has ordained the time both of life and of ruinous death for them, commands me to sing an inspired song. The heavenly God commands me on the one hand, against my will, to announce these things to kings about the empire of Rome …

[7–12] … and a spear, swift Ares, all will be destroyed by him, childish and old he will give justice in the market-places; for there will be many wars and battles and killings of men and famines and plagues and terrible earthquakes and lightning strikes and lightning bolts through-out the entire world, and robbery and the desecration of temples.

[13–20] Then there will be an uprising of the evil Persians, Indians, Armenians, and Arabs at the same time; the Roman king, insatiate of war, will draw near to them, driving warriors against the Assyrians, a new Ares; this warlike Ares will go as far as the deep-flowing, silver-eddied Euphrates, hurling his spear, he will fall in the ranks, smitten by gleaming iron because of jealousy and moreover betrayed by a companion.

[21–34] Then straight away will rule a lover of purple and a warrior, appearing from Syria, the dread of Ares, together with Caesar his son, and he will pacify the entire earth: one name will attach to both of them: upon the first and twentieth five hundreds will be placed. When they will rule in wars and become lawgivers, there will briefly be an end to war, not for long: when the wolf shall swear oaths to the dogs of gleaming teeth against the flock he will ravage, harming the wool-fleeced sheep, and he will break the oaths and then there will be the lawless strife of arrogant kings, in wars the Syrians will perish terribly, Indians, Armenians, Arabs, Persians, and Babylonians will ruin each other in mighty battles.

[35–49] When the Roman Ares destroys the German, defeating the life-destroying Ares of Ocean, then there will be long war for the Persians, arrogant men, and victory will not be with them; for just as a fish does not swim on the top of the cliff of lofty, many-ridged, wind-blown, sun-beaten rock, nor a turtle fly nor an eagle swim in water, even so shall the Persians be very far from victory at that time, as long as the dear nurse of the Italians situated in the plain by the renowned stream of the Nile shall bear the portion of harvest to seven-hilled Rome. The limit for this has been set. For your name contains in numbers the expanse of time allotted to you, Rome, and for that number of years will the great god-like city of the Macedonian king willingly provide you with grain.

[81–8] After him another great-hearted king will rule mighty, flour-ishing Rome, skilled in war, emerging from the Dacians, of the number three hundred; he will be of the fourth race and destroy many, then indeed the king will destroy all the brothers and friends of the slaughtered kings, and immediately there will be spoliation and murder of the faithful because of the former king.

[100–2] … then the king of the Italians will fall in battle, smitten by gleaming iron, in a state of disarray; and his sons will be destroyed with him.

[103–12] When another king of Rome will rule, then ruinous Ares with his bastard son will bring the disorderly races against the Romans, against the wall of Rome. And then suddenly there will be famine, plagues, dreadful lightning bolts, horrible wars, and destruction of cities. The Syrians will be terribly destroyed, for the great wrath of the lord on high will arise against them. There will be an uprising of the evil Persians, and Syrians joined with Persians will destroy the Romans;

but they will not master the things ordained in the divinely wrought plan.

[155–71] When two war-swift lordly men will rule the mighty Romans, one will show forth the number seventy, while the other will be of the third number; and the high-necked bull digging the earth with his hoofs and rousing the dust on his double horns will do much harm to the dark-hued serpent cutting a furrow with its scales; then he will be destroyed. After him again another will come, a well-horned hungry stag in the mountains desiring to feed his stomach with the venom-spitting beasts; then will come the sun-sent, dreadful, fearful lion, breathing much fire. With great and reckless courage he will destroy the well-horned swift stag and the great, venom-spitting, fearsome beast discharging many shafts and the bow-footed goat; fame will attend him; perfect, unblemished, and awesome, he will rule the Romans and the Persians will be feeble.

[172–3] But king, lord of the world, god, put an end to the song of my words, give them a charming song.

10. *Res Gestae Divi Saporis* (after 260)
Original in Middle Persian, Parthian and Greek

[1] I, the Mazda worshipping lord Shapur, king of kings of Iran and non-Iran, whose lineage is from the Gods, son of the Mazda worshipping divinity Ardashir, king of kings of Iran, whose lineage is from the Gods, grandson of king Papak, am ruler of Iranshahr, [and I hold ?] the lands: Persis, Parthia, Khuzistan, Mesene, Assyria, Adiabene, Arabia, Azerbaijan, Armenia, [2] Georgia, Segan [Makhelonia = Mingrelia], Arran [Albania], Balasakan, up to the Caucasus mountains and the Gates of Albania, and all of the mountain chain of Pareshwar, Media, Gurgan, Merv, Herat and all of Aparshahr, Kerman, Seistan, Turan, Makuran, Paradene, Hindustan [India = Sind], the Kushanshahr up to Peshawar, and up to Kashgar, Sogdiana and to the mountains of Tashkent, and on the other side of the sea, Oman. And we have given to a village district the name Peroz-Shapur and we made Hormizd-Ardashir by name Shapur.[3] And these many lands, and rulers and governors, all have become tributary and subject to us. When at first we had become established in the empire, Gordian Caesar raised in all of the Roman Empire a force from the Goth and German realms and marched on Babylonia [Assyria] (Asuristan) against the Empire of Iran

and against us. On the border of Babylonia at Misikhe, a great 'frontal' battle occurred. Gordian Caesar [4] was killed and the Roman force was destroyed. And the Romans made Philip Caesar. Then Philip Caesar came to us for terms, and to ransom their lives, gave us 500,000 *denars*, and became tributary to us. And for this reason we have renamed Misikhe Peroz-Shapur. And Caesar lied again and did wrong to Armenia. Then we attacked the Roman Empire and annihilated at Barbalissos a Roman force of 60,000 [5] and Syria and the environs of Syria we burned, ruined and pillaged all. In this one campaign we conquered of the Roman Empire fortresses and towns: the town of Anatha with surroundings, (Birtha of Arupan ?) with surroundings, Birtha of Asporakan, the town of Sura, Barbalissos, Manbuk, [Hierapolis], [6] Aleppo [Berroia ?], Qennisrin [Khalkida], Apamea, Rhephania, Zeugma, Urima, Gindaros, Armenaza, Seleucia, Antioch, [7] Cyrrhe, another town of Seleucia, Alexandretta, Nicopolis, Sinzara, Hama, Rastan, Dikhor, Dolikhe, Dura, [8] Circusium, Germanicia, Batna, Khanar, and in Cappadocia the towns of Satala, Domana, Artangil, Suisa, Sinda, Phreata, [9] a total of 37 towns with surroundings. In the third campaign, when we attacked Carrhae and Urhai [Edessa] and were besieging Carrhae and Edessa Valerian Caesar marched against us. He had with him a force of 70,000 from Germany, Raetia, Noricum, Dacia, Pannonia, Moesia, Istria, Spain, Africa (?), Thrace, [10] Bithynia, Asia, Pamphylia, Isauria, Lycaonia, Galatia, Lycia, Cilicia, Cappadocia, Phrygia, Syria, Phoenicia, Judaea, Arabia, Mauritania, Germania, Rhodes [Lydia], Osrhoene (?), [11] Mesopotamia. And beyond Carrhae and Edessa we had a great battle with Valerian Caesar. We made prisoner ourselves with our own hands Valerian Caesar and the others, chiefs of that army, the praetorian prefect, senators; we made all prisoners and deported them to Persis. And Syria, Cilicia and Cappadocia [12] we burned, ruined and pillaged. In that campaign we conquered of the Roman Empire the town of Samosata, Alexandria on the Issus, Katabolos, Aegaea, Mopsuestia, Mallos, Adana, Tarsus, Augustinia, [13] Zephyrion, Sebaste, Korykos, Anazarba ([Agrippas]), Kastabala, Neronias, Flavias, Nicopolis, Epiphaneia, [14] Kelenderis, Anemurion, Selinus, Mzdu- [Myonpolis], Antioch, Seleucia, Dometiopolis, Tyana, Caesarea [Meiakariri], Komana [15] Kybistra, Sebasteia, Birtha, Rakundia, Laranda, Iconium, altogether all these cities with their surroundings. And men of the Roman Empire, of non-Iranians, [16] we deported. We settled them in the Empire of Iran in Persis, Parthia, Khuzistan, in Babylonia and in other lands where there were domains of our father, grandfathers and of our ancestors. We searched out for conquest many other lands, and we acquired fame for heroism,which we have not engraved here, except for the preceding. We ordered it written so that whoever comes after us may know [17] this fame, heroism and power of us …

11. Lactantius: *On the Deaths of the Persecutors* (c. 315)
Translated from the Latin

[5.1] And not much later, Valerian, in a not dissimilar frenzy also raised his impious hands to attack god and shed much righteous blood, although for a short period. But god made him suffer punishment in a new and singular way, so that it might be noted for later that the opponents of god always receive the rewards of their evils. [2] Having been captured by the Persian, this man not only lost the power which he had put to improper use, but even his freedom, of which he had deprived others, and lived in the most horrendous slavery. [3] Because Shapur, the king of the Persians, who had captured him, commanded the Roman to bend over and show his back whenever he wanted to step onto his carriage or mount his horse and, having placed his foot on his [Valerian's] back, said reproaching him with a smile, that this was the truth, and not the things which the Romans depicted on boards and plaster. [4] And he lived long under the deserved insults of his conqueror, so that for long the name of the Romans was ridiculed and derided by the barbarians. [5] And this made his punishment even worse, that he had a son who was emperor, but that neither his capture nor his extreme slavery was avenged, and that he was never demanded back. [6] Afterwards, when he had finished his shameful life in such a disgrace, he was flayed and his skin was stripped and dyed in red colour, and placed in the temple of the gods of the barbarians so that the memory of such a splendid triumph might be continued, and this was always shown to our ambassadors, so that when they saw the remainders of their captured *princeps* with their [Persian] gods, they would not trust too much in their own strength.

12. P. Herennius Dexippus: *Scythica* (c. 275)
Translated from the Greek

[F26 (F23)]
Decius, emperor of Rome, was afraid of the power of the Thracians, fearing that a rebellion against his right to rule might come out of it. He wrote them a letter in which he tried to prevent them taking action

against the enemy, concealing the intention behind this thought; he endeavoured to make them alarmed, saying that such unwarlike men should proceed no further nor put to the test their untried courage until help from him arrived.

[F28 (F25)]

'... And wars are decided by endurance rather than by numbers. We have no slight power; 2,000 of us altogether are mustered, and we have a well-fortified post, from which we must make sorties in groups and afflict the enemy, attack them, and ambush them as they pass. By these methods we will gain the upper hand and in this way be powerful, and we will inspire no little fear in the enemy. We will stand against their battle-lines, and the fortifications of this place and the wood will provide no less a defence than weapons.

As our enemies attack from below, they will be harassed by opponents they can hardly see, and they will have to fight against them in a different place, and they will relax their battle formation, and not know where to aim their arrows and spears; even when they fire them they will miss, and instead they will keep being distressed by us. And from our higher fenced-in position we will attack them with a sharp aim, and be fairly safe as we do it, and not easy to stop.

As for hand-to-hand fighting, if it comes to that, you must bear in mind that the greatest danger inspires the greatest zeal, and that in a situation without hope of rescue resistance is all the readier; often what seems hopeless turns out to happen, when men are forced by the impossible and are fighting for reasons which are worthy of effort in hope of vengeance. For there could not be any greater reasons for anger, since our families and city are threatened by the enemy. And those who have been forced to fight alongside them unwillingly may be persuaded to join us if they see our resistance, in the hope of freedom for themselves.

I gather that the emperor's fleet is not far away and is ready to help us, and if we join together with them we will make great inroads. And in this matter I think we will inspire the rest of Greece to this same zeal. I myself am set upon these actions; I won't put myself out of the way of danger or carry out an easier role, my heart is set on glory and I will hazard all: I want to gain for myself the highest sorts of honour and not to destroy my reputation in the city. And I advise you to realise this: death comes upon all men, and to lose one's life fighting for one's city is the most beautiful prize and brings everlasting glory.

And if, after these words, the city's defeat strikes fear into anyone's heart, and he is consequently timid, he should know that most of the other cities were taken through deception on the part of the enemy and were laid waste because of rivalry amongst those who were opposing them. Since it is possible for us to attack the barbarian army if it starts to retreat, or withdraw if it resists, we will jointly bear … they will have to use the passage, and crowded together … we shall be sufficient, we will retreat in safety to the high ground and attack them as they walk, and this will cause the enemy confusion as to what to do about us.

In all likelihood luck will be on our side; our cause, for which we fight the wrongdoers, is most just, and the gods judge here as in most human affairs, since they are very keen to lessen misfortune and to help improve things. It is glorious that we have carried out our inherited role and made these deeds an example of courage and freedom for Greece, and wonderful to have a share in everlasting glory amongst both the living and those yet to be born, showing by our deed that the spirit of the Athenians is not broken in misfortune. We will take as our battlecry our children and those we love the most; let us call on the propitious ruling gods to preserve them, and form up our battle formation.'

This is what he said; the Athenians were much heartened by his words (his speech was a powerful encouragement to resistance), and demanded to be led into battle.

13. Dexippus Inscription (IG II^2 3669)
Translated from the Greek

After petitioning the council of the Areopagos and the council of the 750 and the people of Athens, his children honour the sacrosanct priest Publius Herennius Dexippus Hermeius, son of Ptolemaeus, the rhetor and historian, on account of his excellence. He held the post of king among the six junior archons, the eponymous archonship, he chaired the general assembly and presented games at the great Panathenaion at his own expense.

Cecropia has begotten the best men, very glorious in courage and words, and in the councils, one of whom is Dexippus, who descried the long history of the age and pronounced it precisely; some things he saw himself, and others he garnered from books: he found out the manifold path of history. He was a man of great fame, who stretched his gaze upon infinity and examined closely its long deeds. He had much-lauded fame throughout Hellas, and the new-blown age gave Hellas to Dexippus as the subject of his history. For that reason his children set up their glorious father in stone fashion in return.

14. Odaenathus Inscriptions from *CIS* (after 261/2)
Translated from the Palmyrene

[2.3946]
Statue of Septimius Odaenathus, King of Kings/ and restorer of the whole East, the Septimii/ Zabda, chief of the great army, and Zabbai, general of the army/ of Palmyra, *potentissimi*, erected this for their lord/ in the month of Ab, in the year 582 [August 271]

[2.3971]
For the safety and victory of Septimius
Vaballathus Athenodorus illustrious King of Kings,
Who is also corrector of the entire region, son of
Septimius Odaenathus King of Kings, and also
On behalf of Septimia Bath-Zabbai illustrious
Queen, mother of the sovereign King,
Daughter of Antiochus. Fourteen miles

15. Augsburg Inscription (11 September 260)
Translated from the Latin (*AE* 1993.1231)

In honour of the divine house/ .... of Severus ....

In honour of the divine house./ To the holy goddess Victory for the barbarian peoples of the Semnoni/ or Juthungi on the/ eighth and seventh days before the Kalends of May who were slain/ and put to flight by soldiers from the province/ of Raetia. Also troops from the Germanies and the local population./ Many thousands of Italian captives were freed./ Fulfilling his vows/ Marcus Simplicinius Genialus, rank-holding knight, having the position of commander/ with this same army,/ set up this monument willingly and deservedly./ Dedicated three days before the Ides of Sempember, when our master the Emperor/ Postumus Augustus and Honoratianus were consuls.

In honour of the divine house. To the holy goddess Victory for the barbarian peoples of the Semnoni or Juthungi who were slain and put to flight on the eighth and seventh days before the Kalends of May by soldiers from the province of Raetia, and also troops from the Germanies and the local population. Many thousands of Italian captives were freed. Fulfilling his vows Marcus Simplicinius Genialus, rank-holding knight, having the position of commander with this same army, set up this monument willingly and deservedly. Dedicated three days before the Ides of Sempember, in the year when our master the Emperor Postumus Augustus and Honoratianus were consuls.

16. Inscriptions from *CIL*
Translated from the Latin

[8.2728] Patience. Courage. Hope.

To Etruscus: 'The Salditani, their most splendid city of Saldae and I along with them, ask you, Sir, to encourage Nonius Datus, veteran surveyor of the Third Augustan Legion, to come to Saldae, in order to finish what remains of his work.' I set out and encountered brigands on the roads; I and my companions escaped naked and injured; I came to Saldae; I foregathered with Clemens the procurator. He took me to the mountain, where they were despairing over the useless labour put into an underground passage, and had almost abandoned it, since the boring-work which had been done was greater than the distance across the mountain. It appeared that the tunnels had wandered away from their straight course, so that the higher tunnel had headed right and southwards, while the lower had also headed to its right, which is to say towards the north: so the two parts were wandering apart, having abandoned the straight course. But this straight course was marked out over the mountain from East to West. So that there should be no mistake by the reader regarding the tunnels: the 'higher' is that part where the water runs into the tunnel, the lower that part which it comes out of. When I was assigning the work, I divided it between marines and Gaulish soldiers so that they would all know how to go about the boring process, and they agreed to carry out the joint tunnelling through the mountain in this way. So I had made the measurements, organised the digging of the conduit and undertaken that it should be done according to the plan which I had given to the procurator Petronius Celer. The work carried out, the water flowed and Varus Clemens the procurator dedicated it. Five measures.

So that my work on this conduit at Saldae might be even clearer, I append some letters: from Porcus Vetustinus to Crispinus: 'You have been very generous, Sir, and especially in your kindness and benevolence in summoning Nonius Datus and sending him to me so I could discuss with him the work which he took charge of. So, although I was being urged at the time also to hurry to Caesarea, instead I rushed to Saldae, and inspected the conduit for water that had been successfully begun, but would be a lengthy business, and which could not be completed without the attention of Nonius Datus, who dealt with it both diligently and responsibly. So I would have asked you to allow him to remain with us for some months to carry out the work, if he had not fallen prey to an illness contracted in the course of his excellent hard work.

[13.7844]

[to Iupiter Optimus Maximus]/ and the *genius* of the place for/ the safety of the empire Ma/ sius Ianuari and Ti/ tianus Ianuari have kept their promise freely to the god who deserved it, under the care/of Masius, mentioned above, and of Macer Acceptus, in [the consulship] of Pius and Proclus (= AD 238)

[3.12336] [I] Good Fortune. Fulvius Pius and Pontius Proculus are consuls. 17 days before the Kalends of January. Copied, inspected and completed. From the register of petitions answered by our Lord Emperor Caesar Marcus Antonius Gordianus, Pious, Fortunate, Augustus, and displayed in the portico of the Baths of Trajan, in the words which are written below.

[II] Given by Aurelius Pyrrus, soldier of the Tenth Praetorian Gordian Cohort, Pious, Faithful, in the century of Proculus, of the same village, a householder there.

[III] To Emperor Caesar Marcus Antonius Gordianus, Pious, Fortunate, Augustus, a petition from the villagers of Skaptopara, also known as the Greseitai. You have often, in replying to petitions, announced that in this most fortunate and eternal time of your reign villages should be settled and improved, rather than their inhabitants be ruined. This both results in the security of mankind and benefits your most holy treasury. Consequently we bring a lawful petition to your godliness, hoping that you will graciously give your approval to us as we make our appeal in this way. We inhabit and have our living in the aforementioned village, which is very attractive: it has the use of thermal springs and lies between two of the army camps in Thrace. Because of this the inhabitants remained for a long time undisturbed and without the slightest worry. Wanting for nothing, they fulfilled their taxes and other duties. But when, in time, certain men began to inflict violence and to use force, the village diminished. Two miles from our village there is an official, well-publicised market. People go there to attend the market, which lasts for fifteen days, but they do not stay near the market; they leave it and come through to our village and force us to give them accommodation and much else to support them, without paying any money. In addition to these, soldiers who are being sent elsewhere abandon their route and come to us, forcing us to provide them with accommodation and provisions, without paying any sort of price. Governors with proconsular authority stay with us, largely to use the springs, but these are your procurators. We receive the authorities with the greatest hospitality as we must, but since we cannot put up with the others, we have made entreaties frequently to the governors of Thrace, who have ordered, in accordance with your divine commands, that we must remain unharassed. This is because we have demonstrated that we are not able to submit to this behaviour at all, and instead we have it in mind to leave our family farms because of the violence of those who come to us. We tell you truly that the number of householders has decreased from many to very few.

For some time the ordinances of the governors prevailed and we were not troubled by requests for accommodation or the supply of provisions, but as time went by many people again dared to stick close to us, despising our private station. And so, since we really cannot bear this weight, and since we truly are on the point, like the others, of leaving our family farms, we beg your favour, unconquered Augustus: that you order, by means of a divine reply in writing, everyone to keep to his own road, and tell them not to leave the other villages and come to ours, nor to compel us to furnish them with provisions without charge or to provide accommodation for anyone we don't have to; because the governors frequently ordered that accommodation not be given to anyone unless they had been sent on the service of the governors or procurators. If we do keep being oppressed, we shall flee our homes and the treasury will incur a great loss. So pity us in your divine wisdom and let us remain in our own homes, so that we can pay the holy taxes and other duties. And this will happen for us during your most felicitous reign, if you order your divine words to be written up on a stele and to be displayed publicly. And after we have received this as a result of your Fortune we will be able to express our gratitude, which, holding you in reverence, we feel already.

[IV] Let them recount: Pyrrhus the praetorian came to this meeting by divine benevolence.

It seems to me that one of the gods has favoured the request at hand, since the most divine emperor has devolved the decision about these matters upon you, who was after all the first to have given public declarations and edicts about them; this seems to me to be a work of good fortune.

This was the petition: the village from which the soldier who is being aided lies in the best part of our polity, the city of the Pautaliotes, with a goodly share of mountain and plain; in addition it has hot water spas, which are very suitable not only for pleasure, but also for bodily health and healing. A nearby market is held frequently during the year, and for fifteen days around the Kalends of October it is tax-free, and it transpired that the apparent gains of this village in time turned into losses: according to the aforementioned petition, often many soldiers who were sojourning there would accost the village for hospitality and oppressive services. Because of these improprieties this village, which was previously rather wealthy and populous, has now instead been reduced to the direst of straits. They made entreaties about these things often to the governors, and while the decrees of some of them had effect, afterwards they were entirely ignored through the habitual carrying out of this sort of harassment. Because of this they by necessity fled to the Augustus.

[V] Emperor Caesar Marcus Antonius Gordianus, Pious, Fortunate, Augustus, to the villagers, through the soldier Pyrrhus their fellow householder: this sort of quarrel, directed with entreaties …, ought to be officially settled by the governor's court, which has better knowledge about the matters which will be brought up, rather than by the receipt of an explicit decision in the form of an imperial written opinion. I have written it. I have authorised it. Seals: 7.

17. Ağa Bey Köyü Petition (Severan or Philippian reign)
Translated from the Greek

… 23 in number, as also *frumentarii* … to see … along the thoroughfare … And so that it might seem as though some excuse for such audacity on their part remained, they seized nine men and put them in chains, saying that they would send them to your most excellent procurators, since the most excellent Aelius Aglaus was also carrying out the duties of proconsul. And after the payment of a sum of money, consisting of a ransom for his release of 1,000 Attic drachmas, they let one of the nine go, but held back the remainder in fetters. And we do not know for sure, most holy emperors, whether they will send them alive to the most excellent Aglaus or treat them in the same way as they treated the earlier ones. So we have done as much as wretched men, so cruelly deprived of livelihood and kin, are able, which is to say we have told these things both to your procurator of this administrative region, Aurelius Marcianus, and to your most excellent procurators in Asia. So we are your suppliants, holiest ever emperors, and of your divine reign, which will never be outdone, and are being hindered from devoting ourselves to our jobs of farming: the military police agents and other enemies threaten us, and those of us who are left are in fear of our lives. Consequently, we cannot devote ourselves to working the land, nor, in future, obey the requirement to pay the imperial taxes and levies. We beg that you will graciously accept our entreaty, and will command the governor of the province and your most excellent procurators to punish these misdeeds, to prevent access to the imperial estates, and to stop the trouble which is caused us by the military police agents, who, on the pretext of duties or liturgies, harry and disturb your farmers. For everything which is ours has been since the time of our forefathers liable to the most sacred treasury according to estate law. This is the truth, which is told to your divinity. And if no legal remedy is imposed with your celestial assurance upon those who have carried out these misdeeds, nor is any help forthcoming for the future, then those of us who remain will not be able to bear the greed of the military police agents and other enemies, about which we have entered this plea, and will be forced to leave our ancestral hearths and the graves of our forefathers, and to look for private land in order to keep ourselves safe. For those who behave in this base manner prefer to leave alone those who live there rather than your farmers. We will have to become exiles from the imperial estates, on which we were born and grew up, and on which from the time of our ancestors farmers have continued to keep faith in the emperor's word.

18. Papyrus of Isis to her Family (*Berlin Papyrus* no. 1,680)
Translated from the Greek

Isis to Termuthion her mother, very many greetings. I make supplications for you every day before the lord Sarapis and his fellow gods. I wish you to know that I have arrived at Alexandria safe and sound in four days. I send salutations to my sister and her children, and Eluath and his wife, and Dioscorous and her husband and children … And if Aio wishes to join the army, let him come; for everyone is in the army

19. Command of the Egyptian Prefect (*PSI* 446)
Translated from the Greek

I [the prefect of Egypt] am told that many of the soldiers demand boats and beasts and persons improperly, without having a warrant, when they travel through the country, and that sometimes they seize them by force, and sometimes acquire them from the *strategi*, through preference or flattery. The result of this is that private individuals are subjected to abuse and violence and that the army is blamed for greed and injustice. The prefect commands that no person should ever be given any contribution for travelling without a warrant.

20. The *Constitutio Antoniniana* (*P.Giss.* 40, col. 1.1–12)
The text between square brackets is a later reconstruction
(AD 212), translated from the Greek

Imperator Caesar Marcus Aurelius Augustus Antoninus Pius proclaims: [...] rather [...] the causes and the reasons [...] that I render thanks to the immortal gods for preserving me [when that conspiracy occurred], in that way I believe that I should be able [magnificently and reverently] to appropriately respond to their majesty, [if] I were able to lead [all who are now my people] with all others who should join my people [to the temples] of the gods. I give to all of those [who are under my rule throughout] my whole empire, Roman citizenship, [though the just claims of communities] should remain, with the exception of the [*ded*]*iticii*. Because it is suitable that the [whole populace] ought not only [...] already to share in the victory [...] my edict will expand the majesty of the Roman [people ...]

21. *Digest* (assembled in the sixth century)
Translated from the Latin

[1.3.33 (Ulpian)]
Long custom ought to be observed as right and law for those cases which cannot be traced to written law

[1.3.40 (Modestinus)]
All law is made by consent, or set by necessity or sustained by custom

[1.5.17 (Ulpian)]
Those who are in the Roman world, have become Roman citizens through a decree of the emperor Antoninus [Caracalla]

22. *Damnatio Memoriae* in a Papyrus (*P.Diog.* 3) (AD 209)
Translated from the Greek

Marcus Lucretius Diogenes, son of Marcus Lucretius Minor, from the Hadrianic tribe, from the town of Zenios, about 32 years old, on behalf of his son Herennas, his first year, 16th Poseidon or Toth, in the 18th

year of Severus and Antoninus ~~and Geta~~, our lords Caesar … in the
18th year of (the) Imperatores Caesares Lucius Septimius Severus
Pius Pertinax Arabicus Adiabenicus Parthicus Maximus and Marcus
Aurelius Antoninus, Augusti and ~~[Publius Septimius Geta Caesar
Augustus]~~

23. Oxyrhynchus papyri
Translated from the Greek

[1.77] [First hand:] To Aurelius Ammonius, *gymnasiarch*, in function,
prytanis of the city of Oxyrhynchus, from Julia Dionysia, daughter of
Sarapiacus son of Sarapammon. Since you have asked whether my
house in the area of Temienouthis, which …, in fact belongs to me or
my husband Aurelius Sarapiacus, I swear by the good fortune of Lord
Marcus Aurelius Severus Alexander Caesar that the said house and
everything in it belong to me, Julia Dionysia, in accordance with the
petitions I sent you, and that nothing has been falsified. In the 2nd year
of the Emperor Caesar Marcus Aurelius Severus Alexander, Pious and
Fortunate, Augustus. 24th of Pachon.

[Second hand:] Julia Dionysia swore the oath as above. Aurelius
Diogenes son of Diogenes wrote it, since she did not know how to write.

[1.411] From Aurelius Ptolemaeus, also known as Nemesianus, *strategos*
of the city of Oxyrhynchus. Officials have assembled and charged the
bankers of the banks of exchange with having these closed because of
their reluctance in accepting the divine coin of the emperors. It has
therefore become necessary to issue an order to all bank owners to open
these and to accept and exchange all coins, except those which are
clearly false and forged; and not to them only, but also to all those doing
business of whatever whatsoever. They must understand that if they
disobey this order, they will get the same penalties that in previous years
his highness the prefect appointed to their case. Signed by me, the first
year, Hathur 28

[10.1274] From Aurelia Aristous, daughter of Aurelius Herodes son
of Apion, formerly *gymnasiarch*, council member of the city of
Oxyrhynchus, and from the guardian appointed to me according
to Roman custom Marcus Aurelius Nicocles son of Zoilus, former
gymnasiarch of the same city, to Aurelius Heraclides, also known as
Lucius son of Lucius and whatever else you are called, greetings. The
dreadful announcement has been made to me that my blessed husband

Achillion, also known as Apollonius son of Apollonius, died while he was working as *basilicogrammateus* in the Alexandrian region. Consequently, I acknowledge that I have appointed you by means of this letter to go to Alexandria and to register with his honour the *procurator usiacus* in my name the property of mine and my husband's son, his heir Aurelius Dionysius, also known as Apollonius, who is a *gymnasiarch* of the said city, but still covered by the Laetorian law. The whole is valued at 200,000 sesterces. And I declare that from this property my husband owes me the dowry which came with me when I married him, consisting of gold jewellery, clothes and other items, the total coming to two silver talents and three thousand drachmas … in valuation … thousand five hundred drachmas … was furnishing from … own … two talents and … drachmas … belonging to me … three talents and … drachmas …

[12.1467] [There have long been laws,] most noble prefect, which give those women who are acknowledged to have the right of three children the authority to manage their own affairs and to transact business without a guardian, in the household matters which they carry out, and especially to those women who know how to write. Accordingly, since I am lucky enough to have the honour of so many children, and know my letters so as to be able to write without difficulty, and since this petition should provide more than sufficient assurance, I call on your eminence to allow me to carry out unembarrassedly the household business which I will henceforth set about. I ask that your office deal with it without further discussion as to my rights, so that I might be aided and will forever express appropriate thanks. May you be prosperous. I Aurelia Thaisous, also known as Lolliane, presented this as a petition. In the 10th year, 21st of Epiphi. Your petition has been filed in the office.

24. Inscriptions from Aphrodisias
Translated from the Greek

20. Letter of Gordian III
Emperor Caesar Marcus Antonius Gordianus, Pious, Fortunate, Augustus, Pontifex Maximus, in the 2nd year of tribunician power, consul, *pater patriae*, to the chief magistrates of Aphrodisias, to its council and its people: greetings. It is in keeping with your antiquity, your goodwill and your friendship with Rome, Aphrodisias, that you showed yourself in favour of my reign by means of the decree you passed about me. In return for these attributes and your pious

disposition I am maintaining the definite enjoyment of all your rights which already exist, as they were maintained until the time I took power. Claudius Hegemoneus was the ambassador. Good fortune.

25. Letter of Traianus Decius and Herennius Etruscus
Emperor Caesar Gaius Messius Quintus Traianus Decius, Pious, Fortunate, Augustus, in the 3rd year of tribunician power, consul for the second time, elected consul for a third time, *pater patriae*, proconsul, and Quintus Herennius Etruscus Messius Decius, Pontifex Maximus, in the 1st year of tribunician power, consul elect, to the chief magistrates of Aphrodisias, to its council and people: greetings. On account of the eponymous god of your city, your intimacy with Rome and your good faith, it is fitting that you were delighted at the commencement of our reign, and gave up sincere offerings and prayers. We maintain your accustomed freedom and all the other rights which you have acquired from all the emperors before us, and we are ready to bring to fruition your hopes for the future. Aurelius Theodorus and Aurelius Onesimus were the ambassadors. Good fortune.

25. Acclamation at Perge (*SEG* 34.1306)
Translated from the Greek

Prosper, Perge, which alone has the right of asylum.
Prosper, Perge, to which Tacitus …
Prosper, Perge, made *neokoros* by Vespasian.
Prosper, Perge, honoured with a holy standard.
Prosper, Perge, honoured with silver coinage.
Ephesian Diana, PERGEIAN Diana.
Prosper, Perge, the emperor's treasury. Prosper, Perge, four times *neokoros*.
Prosper, Perge, foremost of the assizes centres.
Prosper, Perge, where consulars compete for honour.
Prosper, Perge, where consulars sponsor games.
Prosper, Perge, crown of Pamphylia.
Prosper, Perge, which tells no lies:
all its rights are confirmed by the senate.

26. The *Feriale Duranum* (Reign of Severus Alexander)
Translated from the Greek

Column I

The Kalends of January: ...

3 days before the Nones of January: because vows are discharged and announced, and for the safety of our lord Marcus Aurelius Severus Alexander Augustus and for the everlasting empire of the Roman people, to Jupiter Optimus Maximus a male ox, to Juno a female ox, to Minerva a female ox, to Jupiter Victor a male ox, ... to Father Mars a bull, to Mars Victor a bull, to Victory a female ox ...

7 days before the Ides of January: because honourable discharge is granted to those who have served out their time along, with the right of privileges; also because salaries are paid out to the soldiers, to Jupiter Optimus Maximus a male ox, to Juno a female ox, to Minerva a female ox, to Safety a female ox, to Father Mars a bull ...

6 days before the Ides of January: for the birthday of the divine empress ..., to the divine ... public prayer.

... days before the Ides of January: for the birthday of Lucius Seius Caesar, father-in-law of the Augustus, a male ox to the genius of Lucius Seius Caesar, father in-law of the Augustus.

9 days before the Kalends of February: for the birthday of the divine Hadrian, to the divine Hadrian a male ox.

5 days before the Kalends of February: for the Arabian and Adiabenine and most great Parthian victories of the divine Severus and for the start of the reign of the divine Trajan, to Parthian Victory a female ox, to the divine Trajan a male ox.

1 day before the Nones of February: for the start of the reign of the divine Antoninus Magnus ..., to the divine Antoninus Magnus a male ox.

The Kalends of March: for the rites of the birthday of Father Mars Victor, a bull to Father Mars Victor.

1 day before the Nones of March: for the start of the reign of the divine Marcus Antoninus and of the divine Lucius Verus, to the divine Marcus a male ox, to the divine Lucius a male ox.

3 days before the Ides of March: because emperor Caesar Marcus Aurelius Severus Alexander was acclaimed emperor, to Jupiter a male ox, to Juno a female ox, to Minerva a female ox, ... to Mars a male ox; and because emperor Caesar Marcus Aurelius Severus Alexander Augustus was first acclaimed emperor by the soldiers ..., public prayer.

1 day before the Ides of March: because Alexander, our Augustus, was acclaimed Augustus, *pater patriae* and *pontifex maximus*, public prayer; to the genius of our lord Alexander Augustus a bull.

Column II

14 days before the Kalends of April: for the day of the festival of the Quinquatria, public prayer; through to 10 days before the Kalends, the same public prayers.

1 day before the Nones of April: for the birthday of the divine Antoninus Magnus, to the divine Antoninus a male ox.

5 days before the Ides of April: for the start of the reign of the divine Pius Severus, to the divine Pius Severus a male ox.

3 days before the Ides of April: for the birthday of the divine Pius Severus, to the divine Pius Severus a male ox.

11 days before the Kalends of May: for the birthday of the eternal city of Rome, to the eternal city of Rome a female ox.

6 days before the Kalends of May: for the birthday of the divine Marcus Antoninus, to the divine Marcus Antoninus a male ox.

The Nones of May: for the birthday of the divine Julia Maesa, to the divine Julia Maesa public prayer.

6 days before the Ides of May: for the Rose festival of the standards, public prayer.

4 days before the Ides of May: for the games of Mars, to Father Mars the Avenger a bull.

12 days before the Kalends of June: because the divine Pius Severus was acclaimed emperor by …, … to the divine Pius Severus.

9 days before the Kalends of June: for the birthday of Germanicus Caesar, public prayer to the memory of Germanicus Caesar.

1 day before the Kalends of June: for the Rose festival of the standards, public prayer.

5 days before the Ides of June: for the festival of Vesta, to Mother Vesta public prayer.

6 days before the Kalends of July: because our lord Marcus Aurelius Severus Alexander was acclaimed Caesar and donned the toga of manhood, to the genius of Alexander Augustus a bull.

The Kalends of July: because Alexander, our Augustus, was first elected consul, public prayer.

4 days before the Nones of July: for the birthday of the divine Matidia, to the divine Matidia public prayer.

6 days before the Ides of July: for the start of the reign of the divine Antoninus Pius, to the divine Antoninus Pius a male ox.

4 days before the Ides of July: for the birthday of the divine Julius, to the divine Julius a male ox.

10 days before the Kalends of August: for the day of the festival of Neptune, immolatory public prayer.

The Kalends of August: for the birthday of the divine Claudius and the divine Pertinax, to the divine Claudius a male ox, to the divine Pertinax a male ox.

The Nones of August: for the games of Safety, to Safety a female ox.

... before the Kalends of September: for the birthday of Mamaea Augusta, mother of our Augustus, to the Juno of Mamaea Augusta ...

... for ...

... before the Kalends of September: for the birthday of the divine Marciana, to the divine Marciana public prayer.

Column III

1 day before the Kalends of September: for the birthday of the divine Commodus, to the divine Commodus a male ox.

7 days before the Ides of September ...

...

14 days before the Kalends of October: for the birthday of the divine Trajan and for the start of the reign of the divine Nerva, to the divine Trajan a male ox, to the divine Nerva a male ox.

13 days before the Kalends of October: for the birthday of the divine Antoninus Pius, to the divine Antoninus Pius a male ox.

... before the Kalends of October: for the birthday of the divine Faustina, to the divine Faustina public prayer.

9 days before the Kalends of October: for the birthday of the divine Augustus, to the divine Augustus a male ox.

[...]

[...]

[...]

[...] of November [...]

[...]

[******]

[...]

[...]

[...] the Kalends [...]

Column IV

16 days before the Kalends of January ..., ... public prayer; through to 10 days before the Kalends the same ...

27. Trajan to Pliny (Pliny: *Letter* 10.97)
Translated from the Latin

You took the course which you should have followed, dear Secundus, when examining the cases of those who were being prosecuted as Christians before you. For there cannot be laid down a universal rule, which would, as it were, have fixed form. They should not be sought out. If they are prosecuted and found guilty, they should be punished, with the provision that he who denies that he is a Christian and makes this clear by action – that is, supplicating to our gods – however suspect his past may be, will obtain pardon for his penitence. Yet petitions put forward without author should have no place in any criminal charge, because they are the worst example, and not of our age.

28. *Libellus* of the Decian Persecution (*Michigan Papyri* 158)
Translated from the Greek

[First hand:] To those in charge of sacrifices in the village of Theadelphia, from Aurelia Bellias daughter of Peteres, and her daughter Kapinis. We have always been zealous in sacrificing to the gods, and now in your presence, according to the orders, I have made a libation, sacrificed, and tasted the offerings, and I ask that you undersign on our behalf. Good fortune.

[Second hand:] We two, Aurelius Severus and Aurelius Hermas, witnessed you sacrificing.

[Third hand:] I, Hermas, sign.

[First hand:] In the first year of the Emperor Caesar Gaius Mesius Quintus Traianus Decius, Pious and Fortunate, Augustus. the 27th of Pauni

29. Cyprian: *To Demetrianus* (252–7)
Translated from the Greek

[3] You have said that all the events which shake and oppress our world are brought about by us, and ought to be imputed to us, because we do not worship your gods. As to that, since you are ignorant of the knowledge of God, and a foreigner to truth, you should know first that the world is now growing old, it does not stand with that strength with which it previously stood, nor does it brim with that force and vigour of which it was once full. Even if we keep silent and proffer no proof from sacred scripture and God's word, the world itself is now speaking and

giving witness to its death with the evidence of general decay. The winter rains no longer provide so much material to nourish seeds; in summer the usual heat which warms the crops is lacking. Spring no longer reaches an agreeable temperature, autumn is no longer fertile with its sprouting branches. Fewer veins of marble are wrenched from the scarred and exhausted mountains; the worked-out mines provide fewer sources of silver and gold, the meagre seams grow smaller every day. The farmer diminishes and weakens in the fields, the sailor at sea, the soldier in camp, as do integrity in court, justice at trial, harmony between friends, knowledge of the arts, discipline as a mode of life. Do you suppose that the world can be as solid as it ages as was possible when it was still young, and that it can prevail in lively youthfulness? It must diminish somewhat now the end is near and it declines towards its final setting. In the same way, the sun when it sinks sends out rays which are less bright and gleamingly afire; the moon grows smaller as its path declines and its horns diminish; the tree which was previously green and fertile becomes sterile and misshapen with old age as its branches dry out; and the spring which used incessantly to pour out abundant streams decreases in old age, until a modicum of moisture scarcely manages to drip out. This is the sentence that the world passes; it is the law of God that everything that is born dies, everything that once grew grows old, everything strong grows weak, everything great declines; and when it has become weak and slight it is finished.

[4] You blame Christians because the pieces of an ageing world fall apart. What if old men too blamed Christians because they were less hale in their old age, because their ears were no longer so good at hearing, their feet at walking, their eyes at seeing, their bodily strength, their organs' vigour, their limbs' power, and because although human life was once lengthy and lasted eight or nine hundred years, it can hardly now stretch to a hundred! We see white hairs on children, hairs that fall out before they have finished growing; life does not finish in old age, but begins with it. So in its very birth the new-born hurries towards its death, so whatever is now born degenerates in the old age of the world itself, and no one should be amazed that certain things in the world are beginning to decay, when the whole world itself is set on failure and death.

[5] So wars continue to be even more frequent, sterility and hunger heighten disquiet, ghastly illness ravages men's health, the human race is devastated by rampaging decay, and you should know that this was

predicted: in the last days evils will be multiplied and calamities will diversify, and as the day of judgement approaches, the censure of an angry God will be stirred up more and more by the arrogance of the human race. For, contrary to your false complaints and your ignorance of the truth, which makes foolish claims and accusations, the things that befall us are not because we do not worship your gods, but because you do not worship God. For he himself is the master of the world and its ruler, and all things are done with his judgement and approval, and it is not possible for anything to exist unless he has made it or permitted it to exist. So when things exist which demonstrate the anger of an indignant God, they do not exist because of us who worship God, but are inflicted by your offences and transgressions, you who do not seek God at all nor fear him, nor set aside vain superstitions and recognise the true religion: that he who is the only God for everyone should alone be worshipped and prayed to.

[8] You complain because the abundant springs, bracing breezes, frequent showers and fertile earth now show you less obedience, because their elements do not serve your uses and pleasures. But it is because of God that all these things serve you, and you are his servant. It is his will that all things are your servants, and you serve him. You yourself exact servitude from your slave, a man compelling a man to serve and obey him, even though you share the fortune of having been born, the same way of dying, you are made of the same bodily material, and have the same rational mind. You come into the world with the same rights and under the same law and later leave it, but if he does not serve you according to your whim, if he does not apply himself to obeying your will, you imperiously and too harshly enforce his servitude: you whip him, you beat him, you afflict and torture him with hunger, thirst, nakedness, and often with chains and incarceration. And yet do you not recognise God as your master when you exercise your own mastery?

[9] So it is appropriate that God does not hold back from striking blows with the whip and inflicting punishment. But if none of this can move nor turn individuals towards God in terror at such disaster, there yet remains the eternal prison, the continuous flame and perpetual punishment. And the groaning of those begging for mercy which comes from there will not be heard, because while they were here, no one paid heed to their fear of an indignant God, who calls out through his prophet and says: hear the word of God, sons of Israel; it is the

judgement of the Lord against the inhabitants of the earth, because there is no pity nor truth nor recognition of God on the earth: malediction and lies and slaughter and theft and adultery are spread across the earth, and they mix blood with blood. For that reason the earth with all its inhabitants, with the beasts of the field, with the serpents of the earth, with the birds of the sky, will mourn, and the fish of the sea will fail, as no one shall judge, no one refute. God says that He is angry because there is no recognition of God on the earth, and God is not known nor feared. God rebukes and accuses the sins of mendacity, lust, fraud, cruelty, impiety, wrath, and no one is converted to innocence. Lo! Those things exist which the words of God predicted earlier, and everyone has faith in the present, not heeding the warning for the future. Even though the soul can hardly recover from the ordeals which constrain and confine it, there is time for wickedness, and despite great peril, for making judgements not about oneself but about others. You are angry that God is angry, as though you deserved some reward for living badly, as if all the things that befall you were not still more minor and slighter than your sins.

[13] What is this insatiable frenzy of torture, this insatiable lust for savagery? Why not rather choose for yourself one decision of two: to be Christian is either a crime or it is not. If it is a crime, why don't you kill those who confess to it? If it is not a crime, why do you persecute the innocent? I ought indeed to be tortured if I deny it. If, fearing your punishment, I were to conceal, with deception and lies, what I was before, and the fact that I did not worship your gods, then I should be tortured, then I should be forced to confess my crime by the infliction of pain, as defendants in other interrogations who deny that they have been justly held for the crime with which they are accused, are tortured, so that the truth of their wrongdoing, which the voice will not act as informer for and express, is revealed by their bodily agony. But now, when I willingly confess and frequently declare, again and again, repeating myself, that I witness myself to be a Christian, why then do you torture me when I confess, when I go about destroying your gods not in hideaways and secret places, but openly, in public, in the marketplace itself, as the magistrates and governors listen. Ought you to hate and punish me more because the evidence against me has grown, even than you did when there was too little to accuse me? Since I announce that I am a Christian in a crowded place, surrounded by people, and I confound you and your gods with a clear and public denunciation, why do you attack the weakness of my earthly flesh? Dispute with the vigour

of my spirit, break the strength of my mind, destroy my faith, defeat me, if you can, with argumentation, defeat me with reason.

30. Cyprian: *Letter* 80 (258)
Translated from the Greek
Cyprianus to his brother Successus, greetings.

[I] My reason for not writing to you straightaway, dearest brother, is that all the priests were fixed here under threat of the arena, and completely unable to leave, all of them prepared for the dedication of their souls to the holy and celestial crown. I sent some men to the city [Rome] to find out the truth about what the emperor had replied about us and bring it back. You should know that they have returned. Many different and untrustworthy rumours were being spread about, the truth of which we now have: Valerianus has replied to the senate that bishops, presbyters and deacons are to be punished immediately, but senators, men of high social standing, and Roman equestrians who have lost their dignity in this way are to have their property confiscated. If they continue to be Christians even after their facilities have been taken away, they are to be executed. Woman should have their property confiscated and be exiled, and any members of Caesar's household, whether they have previously confessed to being a Christian or do so from now on, are to be subject to confiscation, bound, and assigned to Caesar's estates. Emperor Valerianus even added to his statement a transcript of the letters which he sent to the governors of the provinces about us. We are daily hoping these letters will come, since we remain firm, in accordance with our faith, in bearing martyrdom and we hope for the crown of eternal life due to the generosity and indulgence of the Lord.

You should know that Xistus was executed in the cemetery eight days before the ides of August and four deacons with him. But the prefects continue daily with this persecution in the city, and anyone who is brought before them is punished and his goods appropriated by the treasury.

[II] I ask that you make these things known to all our other colleagues too, so that they can everywhere encourage and strengthen our brotherhood, and prepare it for spiritual battle. Thus each of us individually can think of death as nothing but immortality and in total faith and complete virtue rejoice that we are dedicated to the Lord, rather than being afraid when we make our confession; soldiers of God and Christ know this will lead not to our destruction but to our coronation. Dearest brother, I hope you will always prosper in the Lord.

31. *Passion of Perpetua and Felicitas* (early third century)
Translated from the Latin

[10] On the day before we were to fight the beasts, I saw this in a dream: Pomponius the deacon came to the door of the prison and knocked on it vehemently. I went over and opened it to him. He was dressed in a white tunic without a belt and in many-strapped sandals, and he said to me: 'Perpetua, we are waiting for you: come.' He held out his hand to me and we began to go through rugged and winding places. After a little while we came, breathing heavily, to an amphitheatre, and he led me into the middle of the arena and said to me: 'Don't be afraid; I am here with you, and I will work alongside you.' Whereupon he went away. And I caught sight of a huge crowd of intent people; since I knew that I had been condemned to death by wild beasts I wondered why they weren't sending any beasts out to me. And an Egyptian of vile appearance came out opposite me, along with his support team, to fight with me. And beautiful young men came to me, to help and support me. And I was polished, and made a man; and my supporters rubbed me with oil, as fighters are. And on the other side I saw the Egyptian rolling in sand. And a man of incredible size came out: he was even taller than the roof of the amphitheatre, without a belt; he had a purple tunic with two broad stripes across his chest, and beautiful sandals made out of gold and silver. He carried a rod like a *lanista*'s and it was a green branch with golden apples on it. He hushed the crowd and said 'If this Egyptian beats this woman, he will kill her with his sword; if she beats him, she will receive this branch.'

He left, and we approached each other and began to trade blows. He tried to catch hold of my feet, while I struck his face with my heels. And I was carried up into the air, and began to strike him, as if I were not walking on the ground. And when I saw him check I put my hands together, interlacing my fingers, and grabbed his head. He fell on his face, and I trod on his head. The crowd began to shout, and my supporters to sing. I approached the trainer and received the branch. And he kissed me and said to me 'Daughter, peace be with you.' And I began to go to the gate of the living in glory. Then I woke up, and I understood that I would be fighting not against wild beasts but against the devil; but I knew I would be victorious. This statement I have completed as far as the day before the games; someone else must write about what happens at the games, if he wants.

[11] Blessed Saturus too has broadcast this vision, which he himself wrote down. 'We had suffered,' he says, 'and left our bodies, and we began to be carried to the East by four angels, whose hands did not touch us. We did not go turned over on our backs, facing upwards, but as though climbing a steep hill. And when we had left the old world behind we saw a great light, and I said to Perpetua (for she was by my side): "This is what the Lord promised to us: we have received what was promised." And while we were being carried by the same four angels, we came upon a huge area, laid out like a garden, with rose trees and every type of flower. The trees were as high as cypresses, and their leaves never stopped falling. And there in the garden were another four angels, greater than the others. When they saw us, they honoured us and said wonderingly to the other angels: "They are here! They are here!" The four other angels were afraid, the ones who were carrying us, and put us down. So we crossed the area on foot by means of a broad path. There we found Iocundus and Saturninus and Artaxius, who had all been burnt alive as part of the same punishment, and Quintus, who had died as a martyr while still in prison. And we while we were asking them where the others were, the angels said to us: 'First, come along, enter, and pay respect to the Lord.''

[14] These are the rather remarkable visions of the most blessed martyrs Saturus and Perpetua, which they themselves wrote down. But God called Secundulus to a quicker exit from the world while still in prison, not thanklessly, so that he might rob the wild beasts of their prey. Even if his soul did not feel the sword, his body certainly did.

[15] As to Felicitas, the grace of God touched her too in this way: she was eight months' size (she had been pregnant when she was arrested), and as the day of the spectacle approached she was greatly distressed because pregnant women were not allowed to be exposed to punishment, and she did not want hers to be postponed on account of her pregnancy, nor to shed her holy and innocent blood later, along with strangers and criminals. Her fellow martyrs were deeply saddened along with her, not wanting to leave so good a friend, and companion on the road of shared hope, all alone. So three days before the games they all joined together in wailing and poured out prayers to the Lord. Straight after this praying her pains began. While she laboured in childbirth and was in pain due to the natural difficulty of an eight-month birth, one of

the servants of the gaolers said to her: 'If you are suffering now, what will you do when you are thrown to the beasts? You didn't care about them when you refused to sacrifice.' And she replied: 'Now I suffer what I suffer; but then there will be another in me who will suffer on my behalf, because I will suffer for him.' In this way she bore a daughter, whom one of her sisters brought up as her own daughter.

[16] Since the Holy Spirit allowed, and by this permission intended, the events of the games to be written down, even if we are unworthy of entirely describing such glory let us fulfil the promise which was, as it were, the final wish of Perpetua, adding one more witness of her constancy and greatness of spirit. When the tribune harshly punished them, because the warnings of excessively stupid men had made him afraid that they might escape prison through some sort of magical incantation, Perpetua responded to his face: 'Why do you not allow us to regain our strength when we are about to fight the beasts, as punishment for our most notorious crimes, on Caesar's very birthday? Surely it does you no good if we come out on that day too wasted?' The tribune shuddered and grew red, and consequently ordered them to be treated more humanely, and that her brothers and the others should be allowed to come in and rest with them, and the prison assistant now believed.

[20] The devil prepared an extremely ferocious cow for the girls, contrary to the usual situation, in order to match their gender to that of the animal. They were brought out naked and wrapped in small nets. The crowd shuddered, seeing that one girl was dainty and the other had recently given birth and still had leaking breasts. So they were called back, and covered in unbelted tunics. Perpetua was thrown to the beast first, and fell on her loins. When she sat up, she used her tunic, which had been cut off her side, to cover her thigh, being mindful more of modesty than of fear. Then she looked for a pin, and tied up her loose hair; it wasn't appropriate to undergo martyrdom with loose hair, nor should she be seen to grieve in her glory. So she got up, and when she saw that Felicitas had been struck, she went up to her and held out her hand to her, and made her get up. They both stood, side by side, and the cruelty of the crowd was overcome and they were summoned back to the gate of the living. There a catechumen named Rusticus, who was accompanying her, held Perpetua up and she began to look around as if she had been awoken from a dream (this is how much she was in the Spirit and in ecstasy) and said, to everyone's amazement: 'When are we going to be led out to that horrible cow?' And when she had heard what

had occurred, she would not at first have believed it, but for some bruises on her body and cuts in her clothes. Then she summoned her brother, and the catechumen, and said: 'Remain in faith, and love everyone in their turn, and do not be hurt by our sufferings.'

[21] In the same way at the other gate Saturus was persuading the soldier Pudens, saying: 'Altogether, just as I supposed and predicted, I felt not even one wild animal upon me. Now believe with all your heart: look, I am going forward, and I will be eaten by a leopard in a single bite.' And straightaway at the end of the spectacle he was thrown to the leopard, and after a single bite he was wallowing in so much blood that the crowd shouted out to him as he produced evidence of a second baptism: 'Saved and washed, saved and washed.' Evidently whoever had washed in such a way was saved. Then he said to the soldier Pudens: 'Goodbye, and remember my faith and me; let these things not disturb you, but strengthen you.' At the same time he took a small ring from his finger, dipped it in his wound, and gave it to him as an inheritance, leaving a token of himself and a memory of his blood. Thereupon, dying, he was laid out with the others at the place usually used for cutting throats. And when the crowd demanded that they be brought into the middle, so that they could look into each other's eyes as the swords penetrated their bodies, companions in slaughter, they got up voluntarily, carried themselves to where the crowd wanted, and kissed each other before they were killed, so that they might carry out the martyrdom with the rites of peace. Some were motionless, and received the sword in silence; easily the first to give up his spirit was Saturus, who had been the first into the arena, in order to keep back Perpetua. Perpetua herself, in order to taste some pain, let out a cry when she was stabbed between the ribs, and directed the wavering right hand of an apprentice gladiator into her own throat. It may be that such a woman, who caused impure souls to fear her, could not have been killed in any other way, but only if she herself wanted it.

Bravest and most blessed martyrs! Truly called and chosen for the glory of our Lord Jesus Christ! How one must laud, honour and adore them, and certainly one ought to choose these as examples for the building of the Church, no less than the old ones, in order that new virtue may bear witness that it is always carried out by the single and indivisible Holy Spirit, and all-powerful God the Father, and his Son Jesus Christ, our Lord, who has renown and immense power for age upon age. Amen.

32. Marcus Minucius Felix: *Octavius* (c. 210)
Translated from the Latin

[8.1] [Caecilius:] On the immortal gods there has been perpetual agreement by all peoples, notwithstanding everything and though we do not know how to explain them and how they came into being. That is why I do not want to know of those who are so insolent, so confident of their impertinent quasi-wisdom, that they do their utmost to destroy or weaken the old valuable and useful worship as we know it.

[10.4] [Caecilius:] Only the Jews, that horrible people, also know only one god, but they worshipped him openly, worshipped him through temples, altars, ceremonies; but he holds no influence, his power is so utterly unimportant that with his people he is prisoner of the divine powers of the Romans.

[12.5] [Caecilius:] Do the Romans not need your god to force their will on others, to rule as kings, to use all of the earth and be your masters? You, on the other hand, await death in fearful tension and deny yourselves all decent delights. You do not visit spectacles, are absent at processions, feasts for the state lack your presence; you abhor games for the gods, foods of which parts have been given to the gods and drinks of which libations have been poured. In this way, you are fearful of the gods whose existence you deny!

[21.1] [Octavius:] Read the writings of the historians or the writings of wise men: you shall recognise the same things as me. Euhemerus explains that men are deemed gods because of the merits of their virtue or service; he enumerates the birthdays, countries and tombs of Dictaean Jove, Apollo of Delphi, Pharian Isis and Eleusinian Ceres and points them out in the appropriate area.

[21.2] [Octavius:] Prodicus says that those who, in their wanderings, discovered new crops and hence improved mankind's way of life were taken up amongst the gods. Perseus philosophises along the same lines and connects the names of the crops which were discovered with the names of the discoverers of these same crops, as in the line from the comedy: 'Venus is cold without Liber and Ceres.'

[21.3] [Octavius:] Even Alexander the Great of Macedonia wrote a notable letter to his mother, telling a secret about these man-gods betrayed to him by a priest who was afraid of his power. He wrote about Vulcan as the ruler of the world and continued on to the race of Jove, and then wrote how from Isis' corn the myth arose about the swallows, the castanets and the tomb of that Serapis or Osiris of yours, which is empty because his limbs were scattered.

[21.4] [Octavius:] This confirms what we know through others: Saturnus, the first of this race, was after all human, as all Greek and Roman writers of early history tell … But if gods could have children, when they were immortal, then the number of our gods would be greater than that of all humans combined, so that heaven could no longer house them, air could no longer hold them, the earth could no longer bear them. Thus it is clear that they were men, of whom we read that they were born and of whom we know that they have died.

[37.1] [Octavius:] What a magnificent spectacle it is for God when a Christian suffers sorrow, when he is confronted with intimidation, the heaviest punishments and torture, when he laughingly ignores the grinding of Death and the fear of the executioner. When eye to eye with kings and rulers he holds his spiritual freedom high, stepping aside for God alone, to whom he belongs, when as triumphant victor he derides them who sentenced him! He, after all, is the victor who obtained that for which he struggled.

[38.1] [Octavius:] Then there is the fact that we refuse remainders of sacrifices or wine of which part was offered as a libation: that is no admittance of fear, but solemn proclamation of true wisdom; for though all that has come to exist as an inviolable gift of god will not spoil, to whatever use it is put, we still abstain, so that nobody thinks that we yield to the demons to whom libation was offered, or that we are ashamed of our religion

33. Epistle against the Manichees (*P.Ryl.* 469.12-43)
Translated from the Greek

Column I
Again, the Manichees tell lies about marriage: that a man who does not marry is doing right; Paul says that he who does not marry does better, but the fact that fornicators and prostitutes are evil is clear from the holy scriptures: from these we learn that 'marriage is honoured and that God hates prostitutes and fornicators'. So it is clear that he also condemns

those who worship creation, those who … 'debauch wood and stone'. But does he not command that those who do evil be punished? He says: 'if a man or a woman is found in one of your cities, which the lord God gives you, who does evil before the Lord your God, and who worships the sun or everything in the universe, it is an abomination to the Lord your God. Everyone who does these things is an abomination to the Lord God.' The Manichees quite clearly worship creation … in their hymns is an abomination to the Lord.

Column II

'… I did not cast them into the cooking-vessel. Someone else brought these things to me and I ate them without guilt.' From which it makes sense to recognise that the Manichees are filled with great madness. And in particular since their defence of bread-eating is the deed of men who are filled with madness. I have retailed in brief what they claim about these things, from the treatise of the Manichean madness which has come into my possession, in order that we can look out for them entering our houses by means of trickery and lying words. Especially the women whom they call 'elect': they hold these in particular honour because, of course, they need them for their menstrual blood, which they use in their disgusting rituals. We are speaking here of things we don't want to discuss, 'we are not looking for what is convenient for ourselves, but for what will allow many to be saved'. So then, may our all-good and all-holy God allow 'you to abstain from every type of evil': allow to be saved your 'entire spirit and soul and body, blameless in the presence of our Lord Jesus Christ; and others to be welcomed in holy love'. My brothers welcome you alongside me. I pray, beloved, that you will be strong in the Lord, cleansed 'of every defilement of flesh and spirit'.

34. Ban on Magical Consultation (AD 198/9) (*P. Yale*, inv. 299)
Translated from the Greek

I have come across many people who thought that they had been deceived by acts of prophecy, and I have decided that it is immediately necessary, in order that danger should not follow on from their foolishness, to announce clearly to everyone that this sort of dangerous meddling is banned. No one is to claim to know more than is human by means of oracles, documents which are written down as though provided by divine inspiration, processions of the images of the gods, or any other deception of this sort; nor to predict an uncertain future, to make himself available to those who want to learn about it, or to give any sort of answer. If anyone continues to seek this sort of prediction, he should expect to receive capital punishment.

Each of you is to provide for the display of this letter in public on notice boards in the cities and in each village, written in large and easily readable letters. Stay alert to all such behaviour, and if you find anyone practising such forbidden activities, send him in chains to my court. It will not go well for you if I learn once more that you have overlooked such practices in the regions which you administer: you will receive the same punishment as those you protect. For everyone who dares to contravene the above regulations acts alone, but anyone who does not persecute these people with all vigour becomes himself a source of danger to many.

In the 7th year of the emperors Caesar Lucius Septimius Severus Pius Pertinax Arabicus Adiabenicus Parthicus Maximus and Caesar Marcus Aurelius Antoninus, Augusti.

35. Wall of Aurelian

a. Partial view from the air

b. View of the porta Ostiensis

36. Rock Relief at Bishapur

37. Arch of Galerius, Thessalonica (detail)

38. Arch of Septimius Severus, Rome

a. Panel reliefs (detail)

b. Column (detail)

39. Arco degli Argentarii, Rome

a. Panel relief, east side   b. Panel relief, west side

40. Palmyrene Sarcophagus (detail)

41. Syrian Togate Portrait

42. Distribution of Third-Century Imperial Coin Types

Representation of imperial power on Roman imperial coinage, AD 193–284

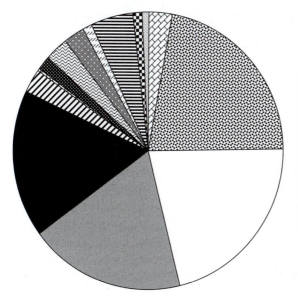

- ▨ Dynastic representation
- ▩ Military representation
- ☐ Divine association
- ▥ *Saeculum Aureum*
- ■ Virtues
- ▰ *Euergesia*
- ⊞ Paradigmata
- ▨ *Restitutor* messages
- ▨ Geographical messages
- ▦ Elevation
- ▨ Non-specific representation
- ☰ *Aeternitas* messages
- ▗ Unica
- ▨ Representation category uncertain

43. Coins of Elagabalus

a. Procession with the sacred stone (218–19)

b. The emperor as priest (222)

© http//www.cgb.fr

44. Trilingual Coin from Tyre (Reign of Gordian III)

45. Coins of Philip the Arab

a. Celebrating the loyalty of the troops (248)

© http//www.cgb.fr

b. Proclaiming the 'Safety of the world' (245)

© http//www.cgb.fr

46. Decius' Consecration Coins (250–1)

a. Augustus

© http//www.cgb.fr

b. Trajan

© http//www.cgb.fr

c. Commodus

© http//www.cgb.fr

d. Severus Alexander

© http//www.cgb.fr

47. Coins of Gallienus

a. Proclaiming the 'Safety of the world' (263)

© http//www.cgb.fr

b. Protected by Apollo (267)

© http//www.cgb.fr

48. Coins of Aurelian and His Opponents

a. Aurelian has reconquered the East (274)

© http//www.cgb.fr

b. Vaballathus and Aurelian (271)

© http//www.cgb.fr

c. Domitian II claims the throne (271)

d. Postumus and Hercules Deusoniensi (260–1)

© http//www.cgb.fr

49. Imperial busts

a. Hadrian

b. Caracalla

c. Macrinus

d. Maximinus Thrax

49. Imperial busts *continued*

e. Decius

f. Gallienus (267)

g. Gallienus (260–5)

Emperors and Usurpers

Roman Empire

Pertinax	193
Didius Julianus	193
Septimius Severus	193–211
Pescennius Niger	193–4
Clodius Albinus	193–7
Caracalla	211–17
Geta	209–11
Macrinus	217–18
Diadumenianus	218
Elagabalus	218–22
Seleucus	?
Uranius	?
Gellius Maximus	?
...s Verus	?
Severus Alexander	222–35
L. Seius Sallustius	225(?)–7(?)
Taurinus	?
Ovinius Camillus	?
Maximinus Thrax	235–8
Magnus	235
(Titus) Quartinus	235
Gordian I	238
Gordian II	238
Balbinus	238
Pupienus	238
Gordian III	238–44
Sabinianus	240
Philip the Arab	244–9
Pacatianus	248
Iotapianus	249
Silbannacus	?
Sponsianus	?
Decius	249–51
L. (?) Priscus	250
Valens Licinianus	250
Herennius Etruscus	251
Hostilianus	251
Trebonianus Gallus	251–3
Volusianus	251–3
Uranius Antoninus	253
Aemilian	253
Valerian	253–60
Gallienus	253–68
Valerianus Iunior	257–8
Saloninus	260
Ingenuus	?
Regalianus	260 (?)
Macrianus	260–1
Quietus	260–1
Piso	261
Valens	261
Mussius Aemilianus	261–2
Aureolous	262–8
Claudius II Gothicus	268–70
Quintillus	270
Aurelian	270–5
Domitian II	271
Urbanus	271/2
Septimius	271/2
Felicissimus	271/2
Tacitus	275–6
Florianus	276
Probus	276–82

Bonosus	280–1
Proculus	280–1
Carus	282–3
Numerian	283–4
Carinus	283–5
Diocletian	284–305

Gallic Empire (260–74)

Postumus	260–9
Laelianus	269
Marius	269
Victorinus	269–71
Tetricus I	271–4
Tetricus II	273–4
Faustinus	273

Palmyrene Empire (260?–72)

(Septimius Odaenathus	260–7/8)
Vaballathus	267–72
Zenobia	267–72
Antiochus	272

Note: Odaenathus did not proclaim himself emperor; see p. 24.

Further Reading

Part I Debates

Introduction

There are only a few accessible introductions providing a narrative framework for third-century history. Most straightforward are Campbell (2005) and Drinkwater (2005), whilst Potter (2004) gives a more in-depth analysis of a much larger stretch of time. Useful brief overviews are included in Potter (1990) and Watson (1999). Still very influential are Alföldy (1974) and MacMullen (1976), for which prior knowledge is, however, advisable. In German, Sommer (2004) is a nice start to the period, though nowhere as complete as two important French overviews: Christol (1997) and Carrié and Rousselle (1999). For all the individual emperors there is the *De imperatoribus Romanis* on-line encyclopaedia of Roman rulers (www.roman-emperors.org). For only some of the rulers do good English biographical treatises exist, such as Birley (1988), de Blois (1976) and Watson (1999). To these should be added, in German, Körner (2002). As always, entries in the *Oxford Classical Dictionary* (1996³) and *Brill's New Pauly* (2002–) are useful for emperors and sources.

The best discussion of Cassius Dio is still Millar (1964), and of Herodian now Zimmermann (1999) (in German). Alternatively, Sidebottom (1998) is of use. The *Historia Augusta* remains problematic, with Syme (1971) a good starting point. The immensity of the subject becomes clear from discussions in the ongoing *Historia Augusta Colloquia*. Bird's translations (1993, 1994) of Eutropius and Aurelius Victor also discuss the authors, as does Eady (1967) for Festus, and Ridley (1982) for Zosimus. On the latter, Paschoud (1971) is superior, but in French. For Dexippus there is now Martin (2006), on Cyprian still Alföldy (1973), both in German. The *Res Gestae Divi Saporis* is studied by Frye (1984), whereas the thirteenth Sibylline oracle is excellently analysed by Potter (1990). On the use of papyri, coins and inscriptions for studying ancient history, much can be learned from Bagnall (1995), Howgego (1996) and Bodel (2001). A well-illustrated overview of third-century sculptural art is included in Kleiner (1992), though Elsner (1998) shows with more insight how Roman art can be used to write history.

Chapter 1: A Capital and its Provinces

The city of Rome in the third century is not often studied, but Curran (2000) is outstanding. What life (and illness) in Rome must have been like for inhabitants of the city becomes clear from Purcell (2000) and Scheidel (2003). For emperors' travels, Halfmann (1986) is seminal. Brigandage is discussed seriously by Grünewald (2004). The various military campaigns are discussed in the general overviews mentioned above. For the eastern campaigns, Dodgeon and Lieu (1991) is excellent, whereas Frye (1984, 2005) is the ideal starting point for the rise and organisational structure of the Sassanid Empire. For interaction between Rome and the various tribes in the Northwest, Drinkwater (2007) is the obvious starting point. Possible climatological reasons for the movement of peoples across the borders of the empire are looked at by Haas (2006). For the Palmyrene Empire, Hartmann (2001) gives the most thorough overview, though in German. In English, a good starting point is the account in Watson (1999). For the Gallic Empire, Drinkwater (1987) is unsurpassed.

Chapter 2: Economy, Armies and Administration

On economic and military changes, and their consequences for the adminis-trative structure of the Empire, much work has been done by de Blois (2002, 2007). Further administrative developments are usefully outlined by Lo Cascio (2005). Millar (1992^2) remains of the utmost importance but is difficult to use without prior knowledge. For general economic developments, with much emphasis on geographical differentiation, the work by Witschel (1999, 2006) is enormously important. Witschel (2004) summarises his main conclusions with a very complete bibliography. Rostovtzeff (1957^2) is seminal, and still illuminating for the ways in which social and economic developments were related in the Roman world. For military developments and the army in general, the best work is by Campbell (2002, 2005b). The third-century petitions are assembled and expertly commented upon by Hauken (1998).

Chapter 3: Law and Citizenship

The literature on the *Constitutio Antoniania* is massive, especially since the 1910 publication of P. Giessen 40 as a fragment of the actual decree. Within recent scholarship, Honoré (2004) interprets the consequences of the *Constitutio* in a legal context, whereas Garnsey (2004) and Mathisen (2006) discuss the consequences in terms of citizenship and identity. For Roman law in the third century, Ibbetson (2005) and Johnston (2005) are a good introduction. As to citizenship, Sherwin-White (1973^2) remains fundamental. The importance of becoming 'Roman' for the stability of the Roman Empire is one of the underlying themes of Ando (2000). What 'becoming Roman' could entail at a regional level in the West is made clear by Woolf (1998); how religious identity could develop in one of the best-known test cases in the

Roman East, Palmyra, by Kaizer (2002). Grubbs (2002) gives essential sources with their context about the position of women in the Roman Empire.

Chapter 4: Development and Perception of Emperorship

On the practicalities of emperorship, especially the notion of the emperor as a person responding to the requests of his subjects, Millar (1992²) is crucial. For the symbolic position of the emperor, Hopkins (1978) is the best short overview, elaborated further by Ando (2000). The relation between Roman art and emperorship is set out by Hannestad (1988), which sets out the groundwork but is on occasions oversimplistic. Modes of analysing the development of imperial representation in the third century through coinage are developed by Manders (2007). The importance of a military reputation for emperors throughout Roman imperial history is clear from Campbell (1984), with the perceptive comments by Hölscher (2003). Roman emperor worship is lucidly (though occasionally controversially) explained by Gradel (2002), though there is still much of value in Price (1984).

Chapter 5: Christianity and Religious Change

The best extensive treatment of Roman religion is Beard et al. (1998), but there are good introductory volumes by Scheid (2003) and Rives (2006). More specifically on third-century religion, Alföldy (1989) (in German) is central. The best-written (and extremely learned) description of the development of Christianity within a pagan context is without doubt Lane Fox (1986). For the causes of persecutions, de Ste Croix (1963) has become seminal. The acts of the martyrs can be read, with commentary, in Musirillo (1972). Understanding intellectual developments in the third century is impossible without looking at philosophers of the time, most importantly Plotinus and Origen. The former is notoriously difficult in his writing, though O'Meara (1993) forms an accessible introduction. The latter is placed in context by Chadwick (1984), who analyses the place of early Christian thinkers in the classical tradition of which they formed part. For world-views in the third-century context in more general terms, Fowden (2005) is an excellent point of departure.

Part II Debates

The following list does not aim for completeness, but rather provides a starting point for further research. It gives a brief overview of accessible translations and commentaries, if any are available.

1. Cassius Dio: *Roman History*. There is a complete parallel translation of Dio's history in the Loeb Classical Library, by E. Cary, which consists of 9 volumes published between 1914 and 1927. It is available on-line at http://penelope. uchicago.edu/Thayer/E/Roman/Texts/Cassius_Dio.

2. Herodian: *History of the Empire after Marcus*. Again, a complete English translation is available in the Loeb Classical Library, by C. R. Whittaker,

published in two volumes (1969–70). There is also a more recent translation in German, by F. L. Müller (Stuttgart 1996).

3. Anonymous: *Historia Augusta*. The *Historia Augusta*, often also called the *Scriptores Historiae Augustae*, was translated for the Loeb Classical Library by D. Magie in three volumes (1921–32) and is on-line at http://penelope. uchicago.edu/Thayer/E/Roman/Texts/Historia_Augusta.

4. Sextus Aurelius Victor: *Book of the Caesars*. The best English translation, with useful historical commentary, is Bird (1994).

5. Eutropius: *Breviarium*. The best English translation, with useful historical commentary, is Bird (1993).

6. Festus: *Breviarium*. The most accessible translation is certainly the 2001 on-line version by T. M. Banich and J. A. Meka at www.roman-emperors. org/festus.htm. See also the edition and commentary by Eady (1967).

7. Zosimus: *New History*. The best English translation, with commentary, is Ridley (1982). Most accessible is an anonymous translation from 1814, probably copying a 1684 translation, available on-line at www. earlychristianwritings.com/fathers.

8. Publius Aelius Aristides: *To Rome*. The complete works of Aristides are translated by C. A. Behr, in the Loeb Classical Library (1973–5) and more recently (1981–6) for Brill (Leiden and Boston).

9. The Thirteenth Sibylline Oracle. The translation used here is from Potter (1990), the only complete English translation of the text, with an extremely useful and learned commentary.

10. *Res Gestae Divi Saporis*. The translation used here comes from Frye (1984). Dodgeon and Lieu (1991) also translates and comments upon much of the text.

11. Lactantius: *On the Deaths of the Persecutors*. The most recent and accurate translation is by J. L. Creed (Oxford 1984). The most accessible translation is in the Library of Nicene and Post-Nicene Fathers, on-line at www.acs.ucalgary. ca/~vandersp/Courses/texts/lactant/lactperf.html.

12. P. Herennius Dexippus: *Scythica*. There is no complete English translation of the work, though Martin (2006) is a very good study, supplying a German translation and commentary.

17. Ağa Bey Köyü petition. A wonderful discussion and translation of many third-century petitions, also including the petition from Skaptopara, is given by Hauken (1998).

21. *Digest*. There are two versions of the seminal translation by A. Watson. The earliest four-volume version also supplies the Latin text (1985), whereas the later two-volume edition (1998) gives an updated English text. Corrections to the translation can be found online at www.iuscivile.com/materials/digest.

23. Oxyrhynchus Papyri. Translations of papyri which are relevant to studying women in the Roman Empire can be found in Grubbs (2002).

24. Inscriptions from Aphrodisias. The documents from the excavation of the theatre at Aphrodisias are translated and discussed by Reynolds (1982).

27. Trajan to Pliny: *Letter* 10.97. There are many English translations of Pliny's letters. A useful introduction is by W. Williams (Warminster 1990). There is also a complete translation in the Loeb Classical Library by B. Radice in two volumes (1968–9).

29–30. Cyprian: *To Demetrianus* and *Letter* 80. The translation of Cyprian's complete works, by E. Wallis, is available in the *Ante-Nicene Fathers*, vol. 5, and at www.sacred-texts.com/chr/ecf/005/0050022.htm.

31. *Passion of Perpetua and Felicitas*. Links to a number of English translations can be found at www.earlychristianwritings.com/actsperpetua.html.

32. Marcus Minucius Felix: *Octavius*. The most recent English annotated translation of this text is the one by G. W. Clarke (New York 1974).

33. Epistle against the Manichees. For this and other Manichaean texts from the Roman Empire, see Gardner and Lieu (2004).

Essay Questions and Exercise Topics

A Capital and its Provinces

Questions

1. Is the building of Aurelian's wall evidence for Rome's weakened position?
2. Was the capture of Valerian by Shapur more devastating in symbolic or real terms?
3. Did the actions of Postumus and Odaenathus strengthen or damage the empire?

Topics

4. Compile a chronological list of battles at the Roman frontiers between AD 193 and 284 (perhaps using *CAH* 12², 772ff.). Compare these with the other troubles facing Rome in the same years. How, if at all, were problems in the centre and at the borders related?
5. Read the *Res Gestae* of Shapur I (**II 10**), and look on the internet for images of Shapur's triumphal monuments. Compare these to the Roman accounts of the wars with Persia. Where do they disagree, and how can we decide who tells the truth?

Economy, Armies and Administration

Questions

6. Is Cyprian (**II 29, 30**) useful as a source for third-century economic history? Why (not)?
7. What was the most important cause of military misbehaviour in the third century?
8. What is the significance of the increase in the number of military men in the imperial administration in the third century?

Topics

9. Catalogue the third-century petitions to Roman emperors (Hauken 1998) and locate these petitions on a map of the empire. Also locate legions and auxiliary cohorts on the map. Can we say that the presence of military units gave rise to problems?
10. Make an overview of third-century economic developments in Italy, Spain or Africa, starting from Witschel (2004). When, if at all, did economic decline set in?

Law and Citizenship

Questions

11. Was the 'great age of jurists' a consequence of imperial behaviour?
12. Who benefited most from the *Constitutio Antoniniana*?
13. How 'Roman' were the new Roman citizens?

Topics

14. Read the text of *P.Giss.* 40 (**II 20**), leaving out the reconstructed phrases. What indications are there that this is the text of the *Constitutio Antoniniana*? Try to find arguments in the modern literature discussing the papyrus. Are these sufficient to identify the text?
15. Assemble evidence for womens' rights outside of Egypt after AD 212 (perhaps starting with Grubbs 2002) and place this alongside Egyptian papyri. Was Egypt exceptional?

Development and Perception of Emperorship

Questions

16. How can Gallienus' different modes of representation be explained?
17. Did busts of emperors show the emperors as they were, or as they wanted to be seen?
18. What was emperor worship for?

Topics

19. Read Dio's account of Augustus' funeral and compare it with Herodian's account of the funeral of Septimius Severus (**II 5 4.2**). What are the essential differences between the two accounts, and how can they be explained?
20. Look at the coins of the emperor Aemilian (*RIC* 4) and fit all coins into the categories mentioned by Manders (2007). How did Aemilian try to portray himself through his coinage?

Christianity and Religious Change

Questions

21. Did Decius have a coherent religious policy?
22. Were persecutions inevitable during the third-century military and economic difficulties?
23. What was the attraction of the oriental cults?

Topics

24. Read Cyprian (**II 29, 30**), the *Passion of Perpetua* (**II 31**), and Minucius Felix (**II 32**). What messages do these texts share? Are these messages by definition the most important ones in third-century Christianity?
25. Assemble anti-Manichaean documents written by Christians. Include the writing of Augustine. Which negative points are stressed most regularly? How can you explain the fierce resistance to Manichaeism by Christians?

General Questions

26. Can the third century be characterised as the rise of the East?
27. What are the problems with Cassius Dio's history as a historical source?
28. How 'Roman' was the empire at the accession of Diocletian?
29. Is continuity or change the dominant factor in the history of the third century?
30. Was there a third-century crisis?

Internet Resources

There is much of value on the internet that deals with (elements of) Rome and its Empire in the third century. Much, however, is also oversimplistic or simply wrong. The following list does not (of course) aim for completeness, but does supply some useful sites to start searching.

General

www.livius.org
One of the largest websites on ancient history, highly accurate and well illustrated. Better on the first two centuries AD than on the third, but with very interesting information on the Sassanids, including beautiful images of Sassanid rock reliefs.

penelope.uchicago.edu/Thayer/E/Roman/home.html (= LacusCurtius: into the Roman world)
As the website itself states, this is a gateway to ancient Rome, with many on-line translations of ancient texts, including the whole of Cassius Dio, and much of the *Historia Augusta*.

www.roman-emperors.org
This is a useful on-line encyclopedia on the rulers of the Roman empire, from Augustus to late Byzantine times. Alongside accurate biographical treatises of the emperors, there are links to maps and coins.

The Sassanids

www.sasanika.com
One of the best sites discussing Sassanid history, providing information on, and many links to, source material and further sites.

www.cais-soas.com
Claims to be the most comprehensive image library of ancient Iranian art, and

has a substantial collection of images of Parthian and Sassanid artefacts and archaeological sites.

Invasions and the Military

darkwing.uoregon.edu/~atlas
This is the site of the 'mapping history' project, which provided Maps 3 and 4 in this book, and has a good module on the third century 'crisis'. It includes interactive and animated representations of military events in the third century, and a wonderful analysis of different factors contributing to the 'crisis'.

www.RomanArmy.com
The largest on-line community of students and enthusiasts of the ancient Roman army. A highly professional site which aims to provide an encyclopedia about the Roman military and has an already impressive database of military tombstones.

Texts

www.perseus.tufts.edu
The Perseus digital library has a classics section, which forms one of the larger collections of on-line ancient texts in translation and the original. Unfortunately less useful for third-century history since it does not include Dio, Herodian or the *Historia Augusta*.

www.thelatinlibrary.com
A large collection of Latin texts, both classical and Christian. It does not provide translations.

Inscriptions and Papyri

www.csad.ox.ac.uk
Website of the Oxford centre for the study of ancient documents, giving an extremely useful overview of links, including on-line corpora of papyri and inscriptions.

www.epigraphische-datenbank-heidelberg.de
One of the on-line databases of inscriptions, which is easy to use.

Coins

www.wildwinds.com/coins
On-line reference and valuation site of ancient coins, with beautiful images of coins for all third-century rulers and most usurpers.

www.numishop.eu
Numismatic auction site, with a large section of Roman coins. It provided most
the images of coins in this book.

Archaeological Finds

www.archaeologie-online.de
Useful and up-to-date website, divided into different categories, and including
much information on and many links to other sites dealing with classical and
provincial Roman archaeology.

Bibliography

Abdy, R. A. (2004), 'The second-known specimen of a coin of Domitian II recorded in a hoard from Oxfordshire', *RN* 160, 219–21.

Adams (1999), 'The poets of Bu Njem: Language, culture and the centurionate', *JRS* 89, 109–34.

Alföldy, G. (1973), 'Der heilige Cyprian und die Krise des Römischen Reiches', *Historia* 22, 479–501 (=Alföldy 1989, 295–318).

— (1974), 'The crisis of the third century as seen by contemporaries', *GRBS* 15, 89–111 (=Alföldy 1989, 319–42).

— (1989), 'Die Krise des Imperium Romanum und die Religion Roms', in Alföldy, *Die Krise des Römischen Reiches: Ausgewählte Beitrage* (Stuttgart), 349–87.

Ando, C. (2000), *Imperial Ideology and Provincial Loyalty in the Roman Empire* (Berkeley and Los Angeles).

Bagnall, R. S. (1995), *Reading Papyri, Writing Ancient History* (London and New York).

Bakker, L. (1993), 'Raetien unter Postumus: Das Siegesdenkmal einer Juthungenschlacht im Jahre 260 n. Chr. Aus Augsburg', *Germania* 71, 369–86.

Balty, J. C. (1988), 'Apamea in Syria in the second and third centuries AD', *JRS* 78, 91–104.

Bassiouni, S. Z. (1989), 'The position of women in Egypt after the *Constitutio Antoniniana*', *International Congress of Papyrology* 19, 229–44.

Beard, M., J. North and S. Price (1998), *Religions of Rome. Volume 1: A History* (Cambridge).

Beck, R. (1998), 'The mysteries of Mithras: A new account of their genesis', *JRS* 88, 115–28.

Bennett, J. (2001), *Trajan: Optimus Princeps* (London and New York²).

Bird, H. W. (1993), *Eutropius: Breviarium* (Liverpool).

— (1994), *Aurelius Victor: De Caesaribus* (Liverpool).

Birley, A. R. (1969), 'The coups d'état of the year AD 193', *BJ* 169, 247–80.

— (1987), *Marcus Aurelius: A Biography* (London²).

— (1988), *Septimius Severus: The African Emperor* (London and New York).

— (1992), *Locus virtutibus patefactus? Zum Beförderungssystem in der hohen Kaiserzeit* (Opladen).

Bleckmann, B. (2006), 'Zu den Motiven der Christenverfolgung des Decius', in Johne et al. 2006, 57–69.

Blois, L. de (1976), *The Policy of the Emperor Gallienus* (Leiden).

— (ed.) (2001a), *Administration, Prosopography and Appointment Policies in the Roman Empire* (= *Impact of Empire* 1) (Amsterdam).

— (2001b), 'Roman jurists and the crisis of the third century AD in the Roman empire', in de Blois (2001a), 136–53.

— (2002), 'The crisis of the third century AD in the Roman empire: A modern myth?', in de Blois and J. Rich (eds), *The Transformation of Economic Life under the Roman Empire* (= *Impact of Empire* 2) (Amsterdam), 204–17.

— (2007), 'The military factor in the onset of crisis in the Roman Empire in the third century AD', in de Blois and Lo Cascio 2007, 497–507.

Blois, L. de and E. Lo Cascio (eds) (2007), *The Impact of the Roman Army (200 BC–AD 476). Economic, Social, Political and Cultural Aspects* (= *Impact of Empire* 6) (Leiden and Boston).

Blois, L. de, P. Funke and J. Hahn (eds) (2006), *The Impact of Imperial Rome on the Religions, Ritual and Religious Life in the Roman Empire* (= *Impact of Empire* 5) (Leiden and Boston).

Bodel, J. (2001), *Epigraphic Evidence: Ancient History from Inscriptions* (London and New York).

Bremmer, J. (2003), 'The vision of Saturus in the *Passio Perpetuae*', in F. García Martínez and G. P. Luttikhuizen (eds), *Jerusalem, Alexandria, Rome: Studies in Ancient Cultural Interaction in Honour of Ton Hilhorst* (Leiden), 55–73.

— (2004), 'The motivation of martyrs: Perpetua and the Palestinians', in B. Luchesi and K. von Stuckrad (eds), *Religion in the Longue Durée: Festschrift für Hans G. Knippenberg zu seinem 65. Geburtstag* (Berlin and New York), 535–54.

Burkert, W. (1987), *Ancient Mystery Cults* (Cambridge, MA, and London).

Busch, A. (2007), '*Militia in urbe*: The military presence in Rome', in de Blois and Lo Cascio 2007, 315–41.

Butler, R. D. (2006), *The New Prophecy and New Visions: Evidence of Montanism in The Passion of Perpetua and Felicitas* (Washington, DC).

Campbell, J. B. (1984), *The Emperor and the Roman Army, 31 BC–AD 235* (Oxford).

— (2002), *Warfare and Society in Imperial Rome, 31 BC–AD 280* (London and New York).

— (2005a), 'The Severan dynasty', *CAH* 12² (Cambridge), 1–27.

— (2005b), 'The army', *CAH* 12² (Cambridge), 110–30.

Carlisle, E. J. and J. S. Carlisle (1920), 'Septimius Severus (Negro emperor of Rome)', in Carlisle and Carlisle, *Historical Sketches of the Ancient Negro: A Compilation* (London), 76–97.

Carrié, J.-M. and A. Rousselle (1999), *L'empire romain en mutation des Sévères à Constantin* (Paris), 192–337.

Cartwright, F. F. (1972), *Disease and History* (New York).

Chadwick, H. (1984), *Early Christian Thought and the Classical Tradition: Studies in Justin, Clement and Origen* (Oxford).

Christol, M. (1986), *Essai sur l'évolution des carrières sénatoriales dans la 2e moitié du IIe s. ap. J.-C.* (Paris).

— (1997), *L'empire romain du troisième siècle* (Paris).

Clarke, G. (2005), 'Christianity in the first three centuries', *CAH* 12² (Cambridge), 589–671.

Cotton, H. (1993), 'The guardianship of Jesus son of Babatha: Roman and local law in the province of Arabia', *JRS* 83, 94–108.

Cumont, F. (1911), *The Oriental Religions in Roman Paganism* (Chicago).

Curran, J. R. (2000), *Pagan City and Christian Capital: Rome in the Fourth Century* (Oxford).

Dodds, E. R. (1965), *Pagan and Christian in an Age of Anxiety: Some Aspects of Religious Experience from Marcus Aurelius to Constantine* (New York).

Dodgeon, M. H. and S. N. C. Lieu (eds) (1991), *The Roman Eastern Frontier and the Persian Wars AD 226–363. A Documentary History* (London and New York).

Drinkwater, J. F. (1987), *The Gallic Empire: Separatism and Continuity in the North-Western Provinces of the Roman Empire AD 260–272* (Stuttgart).

— (2005), 'Maximinus to Diocletian and the "crisis"', *CAH* 12² (Cambridge), 28–66.

— (2007), *The Alamanni and Rome* (Oxford).

Duncan-Jones, R. P. (1996,) 'The impact of the Antonine plague', *JRA* 9, 108–36.

— (2004), 'Economic change and the transition to Late Antiquity', in Swain and Edwards 2004, 20–52.

Eady, J. W. (1967), *The Breviarium of Festus* (London).

Eck, W. (2007), 'Krise oder Nichtkrise – das ist hier die Frage: Köln und sein Territorium in der 2. Hälfte des 3. Jahrhunderts', in Hekster et al. 2007, 23–43.

Elsner, J. (1998), *Imperial Rome and Christian Triumph* (Oxford).

Fowden, G. (2005), 'Late polytheism: The world view', *CAH* 12² (Cambridge), 521–37.

Fowler, R. and O. Hekster (2005), 'Imagining kings: From Persia to Rome', in Hekster and Fowler 2005, 9–38.

Frier, B. W. (1982), 'Roman life expectancy: Ulpian's evidence', *HSCP* 86, 213–51.

— (1999), 'Roman demography', in D. S. Potter and D. J. Mattingly (eds), *Life, Death and Entertainment in the Roman Empire* (Ann Arbor, MI), 85–109.

Frye, R. N. (1984), *The History of Ancient Iran* (Munich).

— 2005, 'The Sassanians', *CAH* 12² (Cambridge), 461–80.

Gardner, I. and S. N. C. Lieu (2004), *Manichaean Texts from the Roman Empire* (Cambridge).

Garnsey, P. (2004), 'Roman citizenship and Roman law in the late empire', in Swain and Edwards 2004, 133–55.

Gibbon, E. (1776–88), *The History of the Decline and Fall of the Roman Empire* (London).

Gordon, R. (1994), 'Who worshipped Mithras?', *JRA* 7, 459–74.

Gordon, R., J. Reynolds, M. Beard and C. Roueché (1997), 'Roman inscriptions 1991–95', *JRS* 87, 203–40.

Gradel, I. (2002), *Emperor Worship and Roman Religion* (Oxford).

Griffin, M. (1984), *Nero: The End of a Dynasty* (London).

Grig, L. (2004), *Making Martyrs in Late Antiquity* (London).

Grubbs, J. E. (2002), *Women and Law in the Roman Empire: A Sourcebook on Marriage, Divorce and Widowhood* (London and New York).

Grünewald, T. (2004), *Bandits in the Roman Empire: Myth and Reality* (London and New York).

Haas, J. (2006), *Die Umweltkrise des 3. Jahrhunderts n. Chr. Im Nordwesten des Imperium Romanum: Interdisziplinäre Studien zu einem Aspekt der allgemeinen Reichskrise im Bereich der beiden Germaniae sowie der Belgicae unde der Raetiae* (Stuttgart).

Haegemans, K. (2003), 'Representation and perception of imperial power in AD 238: The numismatic evidence', in L. de Blois, P. Erdkamp, O. Hekster, G. de Klein and S. Mols (eds), *The Representation and Perception of Roman Imperial Power* (= *Impact of Empire* 3) (Amsterdam), 466–80.

Haensch, R. (2006), 'Pagane Priester des römischen Heeres im 3. Jahrhundert nach Christus', in de Blois et al. 2006, 208–18.

Halfmann, H. (1979), *Die Senatoren aus dem östlichen Teil des Imperium Romanum bis zum Ende des 2. Jh. N. Chr.* (Göttingen).

— (1986), *Itinera principum: Geschichte und Typologie der Kaiserreisen im Römischen Reich* (Stuttgart).

Hannestad, N. (1988), *Roman Art and Imperial Policy* (Aarhus).

Hartmann, U. (2001), *Das palmyrenische Teilreich* (Stuttgart).

Hauken, T. (1998), *Petition and Response: An Epigraphic Study of Petitions to Roman Emperors 181–249* (Bergen).

Hekster, O. (1999), 'The city of Rome in late imperial ideology: The Tetrarchs, Maxentius and Constantine', *Mediterraneo Antico* II.2, 717–48.

— (2002), *Commodus: An Emperor at the Crossroads* (Amsterdam).

— (2007), 'Fighting for Rome: The emperor as a military leader', in de Blois and Lo Cascio 2007, 91–105.

Hekster, O. and R. Fowler (eds) (2005), *Imaginary Kings: Royal Images in the Ancient Near East, Greece and Rome* (Stuttgart).

Hekster, O. and E. Manders (2006), 'Kaiser gegen Kaiser: Bilder der Macht im 3. Jahrhunderts', in Johne et al. 2006, 135–44.

Hekster, O., G. de Kleijn and D. Slootjes (eds) (2007), *Crises and the Roman Empire* (= *Impact of Empire* 7) (Leiden and Boston).

Henrichs, A. and L. Koenen (1982), 'Der Kölner Mani-Codex (P. Colon. inv. nr.

4780) PERI THS GENNHS TOU SWMATOS AUTOU: Edition der Seiten 121–192', *ZPE* 48, 1–59.

Hölscher, T. (2003), 'Images of war in Greece and Rome: Between military practice, public memory, and cultural symbolism', *JRS* 93, 1–17.

Homo, L. (1913), 'L'empereur Gallien et la crise de l'Empire romain au IIIe siècle', *Revue Historique* 113, 1–22; 225–67.

Honoré, A. M. (1982), *Ulpian* (Oxford).

— (2004), 'Roman law AD 200–400: From cosmopolis to Rechtstaat?', in Swain and Edwards 2004, 109–32.

Hopkins, K. (1978), *Conquerors and Slaves: Sociological Studies in Roman History* 1 (Cambridge).

— (1998), 'Christian number and its implications', *Journal of Early Christian Studies* 6, 185–226.

Howgego, C. (1996), *Ancient History from Coins* (London and New York).

— (2005), 'Coinage and identity in the Roman provinces', in C. Howgego, V. Heuchert and A. Burnett (eds), *Coinage and Identity in the Roman Provinces* (Oxford), 1–27.

Ibbetson, D. (2005), 'High classical law', *CAH* 12² (Cambridge), 184–99.

Icks, M. (2006), 'Priesthood and imperial power: The religious reforms of Heliogabalus, 220–222 AD', in de Blois et al. 2006, 169–78.

Isaac, B. 1988, 'The meaning of the terms *limes* and *limitanei*', *JRS* 78, 125–47.

Jaillet, P. (1996), 'Les dispositions du Code Théodosien sur les terres aban-données', in J.-L. Fiches (ed.), *Le IIIe siècle en Gaule Narbonnaise: Données régionales sur la crise de l'Empire* (Antibes), 333–404.

Jehne, M. (1996), 'Überlegungen zur Chronologie der Jahre 259–261 n. Chr. im Lichte der neuen Postumus-Inschrift aus Augsburg', *Bayrische Vorge-schichtsblätter* 61, 185–206.

Johne, K.-P., T. Gerhardt and U. Hartmann (eds) (2006), *Deleto paene imperio Romano: Transformationsprozesse des Römischen Reiches im 3. Jahrhundert und ihre Rezeption in der Neuzeit* (Stuttgart).

Johnston, D. (2005), 'Epiclassical law', *CAH* 12² (Cambridge), 200–7.

Jones, E. L. (1972), 'Lucius Septimius Severus (145–211 AD): The black emperor of the world (193–211 AD)', in Jones, *Profiles in African Heritage* (Seattle), 129–50.

Jong, J. de (2007), 'Propaganda or pragmatism? *Damnatio memoriae* in the third-century *papyri* and imperial representation', in S. Benoist (ed.), *Mémoire et histoire: Les procedures de condemnation dans l'Antiquité romaine* (Metz), 94–111.

Jongman, W. (2007), 'Gibbon was right: The decline and fall of the Roman economy', in Hekster et al. 2007, 183–99.

Kaizer, T. (2002), *The Religious Life of Palmyra* (Stuttgart).

Kleiner, D. E. E. (1992), *Roman Sculpture* (New Haven, CT, and London).

Knipfing, J. R. (1923), 'The *libelli* of the Decian persecution', *HTR* 16, 345–90.

Körner, C. (2002), *Philippus Arabs, ein Soldatenkaiser in der Tradition des antoninisch- severischen Prinzipats* (Berlin and New York).

Lane Fox, R. (1986), *Pagans and Christian in the Mediterranean World from the Second Century AD to the Conversion of Constantine* (London).

Levick, B. (1999), 'Messages on the Roman coinage: Types and inscriptions', in G. M. Paul and M. Ierardi (eds), *Roman Coins and Public Life under the Empire: E. Togo Salmon Papers II* (Ann Arbor, MI), 41–60.

Liebeschuetz, W. (2007), 'Was there a crisis of the third century?', in Hekster et al. 2007, 11–20.

Lieu, S. (1985), *Manichaeism in the Later Roman Empire and Medieval China: A Historical Survey* (Manchester).

Lo Cascio, E. (2005), 'The emperor and his administation', *CAH* 12² (Cambridge), 131–83.

MacMullen, R. (1976), *Roman Government's Response to Crisis, AD 235–337* (New Haven, CT, and London).

— (1981), *Paganism in the Roman Empire* (New Haven, CT, and London).

— (1982), 'The epigraphic habit in the Roman Empire', *American Journal of Philology* 103, 233–46.

— (1988), *Corruption and the Decline of Rome* (New Haven, CT, and London).

Manders, E. (2007), 'Mapping the representation of Roman imperial power in times of crises', in Hekster et al. 2007, 275–90.

Martin, G. (2006), *Dexipp von Athen: Edition, Übersetzung und begleitende Studien* (Tübingen).

Mathisen, R. W. (2006), '*Peregrini, barbari,* and *cives Romani*: Concepts of citizenship and the legal identity of barbarians in the later Roman Empire', *American Historical Review* 111, 1011–39.

Mattingly, D. J. and R. B. Hitchner (1995), 'Roman Africa: An archaeological survey', *JRS* 85, 165–213.

Mennen, I. (2007), 'The Caesonii in the third century AD: The impact of crises on senatorial status and power', in Hekster et al. 2007, 111–24.

Millar, F. (1964), *A Study of Cassius Dio* (Oxford).

— (1969), 'P.Herennius Dexippus: The Greek world and the third-century invasions', *JRS* 59, 13–29 (= Millar 2004, 265–97).

— (1973), 'The imperial cult and the persecutions', in W. den Boer (ed.), *Le culte des souverains dans l'empire romain* (Geneva), 145–65 (= Millar 2004, 298–312).

— (1981), *The Roman Empire and its Neighbours* (London²).

— (1982), 'Emperors, frontiers, and foreign relations, 31 BC to AD 378', *Britannia* 13, 1–23 (= Millar 2004, 160–94).

— (1992), *The Emperor in the Roman World* (London²).

— (1993), *The Roman Near East, 31 BC–AD 337* (Cambridge, MA, and London).

— (1999), 'The Greek East and Roman law: the dossier of M. Cn. Licinius Rufinus', *JRS* 89, 90–108 (= Millar 2004, 435–64).

— (2004), *Government, Society and Culture in the Roman Empire* (= *Rome, the Greek World, and the East*, vol. 2) (Chapel Hill, NC, and London).

Musirillo, H. (1972), *The Acts of the Christian Martyrs* (Oxford).

Noreña, C. F. (2001), 'The communication of the emperor's virtues', *JRS* 91, 146–68.

North, J. (1992), 'The development of religious pluralism', in S. Lieu, J. North and T. Rajak (eds), *The Jews among Pagans and Christians in the Roman Empire* (London and New York), 174–93.

O'Meara, D. J. (1993), *Plotinus: An Introduction to the Enneads* (Oxford).

Paschoud, F. (1971), *Zosime: Histoire Nouvelle* (Paris).

Peachin, M. (1996), Iudex vice sacra: *Deputy Emperors and the Administration of Justice during the Principate* (Stuttgart).

Pekáry, T. (1987), '*Seditio*: Unruhen und Revolten im römischen Reich von Augustus bis Commodus', *AncSoc* 18, 133–50.

Pestman, P. W. (1994), *Les papyrus démotiques de Tsenhor: Les archives privées d'une femme egyptienne du temps de Darius 1er. Textes* (Paris).

Potter, D. S. (1990), *Prophecy and History in the Crisis of the Roman Empire: A Historical Commentary on the Thirteenth Sibylline Oracle* (Oxford).

— (2004), *The Roman Empire at Bay,* AD *180–395* (London and New York).

Price, S. R. F. (1984), *Ritual and Power: The Roman Imperial Cult in Asia Minor* (Cambridge).

Purcell, N. (2000), 'Rome and Italy', *CAH* 11^2 (Cambridge), 405–43.

Rathbone, D. W. (1996), 'Monetisation, not price inflation, in third century AD Egypt', in C. E. King and D. Wigg (eds), *Coin Finds and Coin Use in the Roman World* (Berlin), 321–39.

Rea, J. R. (1972), *Oxyrhynchus Papyri XL* (London).

Rees, R. (2004), *Diocletian and the Tetrarchy: Debates and Documents in Ancient History* (Edinburgh).

Reynolds, J. (1982), *Aphrodisias and Rome: Documents from the Excavation of the Theatre at Aphrodisias Conducted by Professor Kenan T. Erim Together with Some Related Texts* (London).

Ridley, R. T. (1982), *Zosimus: New History* (Canberra).

Rives, J. B. (1999), 'The decree of Decius and the religion of empire', *JRS* 89, 135–54.

— (2006), *Religion in the Roman Empire* (Oxford).

Rostovtzeff, M. I. (1923), 'La crise sociale et politique de l'Empire Romain au IIIe siècle aprè J.-C.', *Musée Belge* 27, 233–42.

— (1957), *Social and Economic History of the Roman Empire* (Oxford^2).

Roueché, C. (1984), 'Acclamations in the later Roman Empire: New evidence from Aphrodisias', *JRS* 74, 181–99.

— (1989), '*Floreat Perge*', in M. M. MacKenzie and Roueché (eds), *Images of Authority: Papers Presented to Joyce Reynolds on the Occasion of her 70th Birthday* (Cambridge), 206–28.

Rubin, Z. (1995), 'Mass movement in Late Antiquity', in L. Malkin and W. Z. Rubinsohn (eds), *Leaders and Masses in the Roman World: Studies in Honor of Zvi Yavetz* (Leiden, New York and Cologne), 129–87.

Salway, B. (1994), 'What's in a name? A survey of Roman onomastic practice from c. 700 BC to AD 700', *JRS* 84, 124–45.

Sasse, C. (1962), 'Literaturübersicht zur C.A.', *JJP* 14, 109–49.

Scheid, J. (1998), 'Déchiffres de monnaies. Réflexions sur la representation figurée des Jeux séculaires', in C. Auvray-Assayas (ed.), *Images romaines* (Paris), 13–35.

— (2003), *An Introduction to Roman Religion* (Bloomington, IN).

Scheidel, W. (2003), 'Germs for Rome', in C. Edwards and G. Woolf (eds), *Rome the Cosmopolis* (Cambridge), 158–76.

Schmidt-Colinet, A. and K. al-As'ad (in press), 'Zwei Neufunde Palmyrenischer Sarkophage', in G. Koch (ed.), *Symposium des Sarkophag-Corpus, Marburg 2001* (Marburg).

Shaw, B. D. (1993), 'The passion of Perpetua', *Past and Present* 139, 3–45.

Sherwin-White, A. N. (1973), *The Roman Citizenship* (Oxford²).

Sidebottom, H. (1998), 'Herodian's historical methods and understanding of history', *ANRW* II.34.4, 2775–836.

Simon, E. (1995), 'Die constitution Antoniniana und ein syrischer Porträt', in C. Schubert and K. Brodersen (eds), *Rom und der griechische Osten: Festschrift für Hatto H. Schmitt zum 65. Geburtstag, dargebracht von Schülern, Freunden und Münchener Kollegen* (Stuttgart), 249–50.

Sommer, M. (2004), *Die Soldatenkaiser* (Darmstadt).

Speidel, M. P. (1975), 'The rise of ethnic units in the Roman imperial army', *ANRW* 2.3, 202–31.

Speidel, M. A. (1992), 'Roman army pay scales', *JRS* 82, 87–106.

Ste Croix, G. E. M. de (1963), 'Why were the early Christians persecuted?', *Past and Present* 26, 6–38 (= M. I. Finley (ed.) (1979), *Studies in Ancient Society* (London), 210–49).

Stolte, B. (2001), 'The impact of Roman law in Egypt and the Near East in the third century AD: The documentary evidence', in de Blois 2001a, 167–79.

Strobel, K. (1993), *Das Imperium Romanum in '3. Jahrhundert': Modell einer historischen Krise* (Stuttgart).

Swain, S. and M. Edwards (eds) (2004), *Approaching Late Antiquity: The Transformation from Early to Late Empire* (Oxford).

Syme, R. (1970), 'Three jurists', *Bonner Historia-Augusta-Colloquium 1968/9* (Bonn), 309–23 (= *Roman Papers* II, 1979, 790–804).

— (1971), *Emperors and Biography* (Oxford).

Verboven, K. (2007), 'Demise and fall of the Augustan monetary system', in Hekster et al. 2007, 245–57.

Walbank, F. W. (1969), *The Awful Revolution: The Decline of the Roman Empire in the West* (Liverpool).

Watson, A. (1999), *Aurelian and the Third Century* (London and New York).

Weigel, R. (1990), 'Gallienus' "animal series" coins and Roman religion', *Numismatic Chronicle* 150, 135–43.

Witschel, C. (1999), *Krise – Rezession – Stagnation: Der Westen des römischen*

Reiches im 3. Jahrhundert n. Chr. (Frankfurt).

— (2004), 'Re-evaluating the Roman West in the 3rd c. AD', *JRA* 17, 251–81.

— (2006), 'Zur Situation im römischen Africa während des 3. Jahrhunderts', in Johne et al. 2006, 145–221.

Woolf, G. (1998), *Becoming Roman: The Origins of Provincial Civilization in Gaul* (Cambridge).

Zanker, P. (2004), *Die Apotheose der römischen Kaiser* (Munich).

Zimmermann, M. (1999), *Kaiser und Ereignis: Studien zum Geschichtswerk Herodians* (Munich).

Zwalve, W. (2001), '*In re* Iulius Agrippa's estate: Q. Cervidius Scaevola, Iulia Doman and the estate of Iulius Agrippa', in de Blois 2001a, 154–66.

— (2007), '*Codex Justinianus* 6.21.1: Florus's case', in Hekster et al. 2007, 367–78.

Glossary

ab epistulis	Official responsible for the imperial correspondence
adlocutio	Address of an army commander to the military
aequitas	Tranquillity, justice
aeternitas	Eternity
ala	Auxiliary cavalry regiment
amici	(Political) friends
anachoresis	Land flight to avoid taxation
angareia	See *vehiculatio*
aureus	Gold coin; the most valuable Roman denomination
basilicogrammateus	Deputy of a *strategos*
colonia	Roman colony, in the later empire an honorific title for cities in the Roman Empire
comitatus	Special cavalry unit, which was independent of the legions and directly linked to the emperor in person
concordia militum	Military unity
conservator Augusti	Preserver or defender of the emperor
cursus honorum	Career ladder of the Roman elite
damnatio memoriae	Condemnation of the memory of a deceased person
denarius	Silver coin
divi	Deified emperors
dux	Military officer commanding a garrison
epitome	'Highlight'; a later condensed version of an earlier text
euergesia	Beneficence
fiscus	Property of the emperor, imperial treasury
frumentarii	Roman secret service
gymnasiarch	Official in charge of a *nome* capital
hostis	Enemy of the Roman state
iudex vice sacra	Deputy-emperor
ius civile	Roman civil law
ius gentium	Laws applying to non-Romans, defining their relation to Roman citizens
ius liberorum	Right to act without a guardian
lanista	Manager/owner of a gladiatorial training school

legatus	Magistrate sent by the emperor to command a province
legio	Legion
neokoros	City with a temple for the imperial cult
nome	Administrative area in Egypt, usually consisting of a metropolis and surrounding countryside
pater patriae	Father of his country
pax deorum	Peaceful relation between gods and men
pax Romana	The Roman peace
perfectissimus	Most excellent (honorary title)
pontifex maximus	Chief priest of Rome
potentissimi	Most powerful (honorary title)
praefectus praetorio	Prefect (commander) of the praetorian guard, the only armed troops in the Italian peninsula
praefectus urbi	Prefect (commander) of the city of Rome, responsible for maintaining order in the city
princeps	Emperor
procurator usiacus	Roman knight, based in Alexandria, supervising the imperial domains in Egypt
providentia	Foresight
prytanis	Official who was responsible for appointing men to take up public office
rationalis	Treasurer
restitutor	Restorer
Saeculum Aureum	Golden Age
securitas orbis	Safety of the world
strategos	Official in charge of the administration of a *nome*
vehiculatio	A system which obliged provincial subjects to provide transportation and lodging for official Roman travellers based in the provinces
virtus	Manly courage

Index